Reading Shakespeare can be a real headache

That's why we've put this book together.

We've put notes handily next to the play so you don't have to go hunting for "Note 136". That means you can understand what all the weird bits mean without losing the flow of the play.

We've written the notes in plain English to make it just that bit easier.

There's even the odd bit of ever-so-nearly entertaining humour in the notes and pictures to help you breeze through the toughest of scenes.

We've done our bit — the rest is up to you.

What CGP is all about

Our sole aim here at CGP is to produce the highest quality books — carefully written, immaculately presented and dangerously close to being funny.

Then we work our socks off to get them out to you — at the cheapest possible prices.

CONTENTS

Act 4

Act 5

Published by CGP

Editors:
Taissa Csáky
Charley Darbishire
John Kitching
Tim Major
Katherine Reed
Ed Robinson
Emma Stevens

With thanks to Ed Robinson, Keri Barrow and Paula Barnett for the proofreading.

ISBN: 978 1 84146 531 9

Groovy website: www.cgpbooks.co.uk

Jolly bits of clipart from CorelDRAW®

Printed by Elanders Ltd, Newcastle upon Tyne.

Based on the classic CGP style created by Richard Parsons.

Photocopying – it's dull, grey and sometimes a bit naughty. Luckily, it's dead cheap, easy and quick to
order more copies of this book from CGP – just call us on 0870 750 1242. Phew!

ACT 1 SCENE 1
Before Leonato's house

Enter LEONATO, HERO *and* BEATRICE,
with a MESSENGER

A messenger comes to tell Leonato that Don Pedro's won the war against his brother Don John. They've made up and they're coming to visit, along with their supporters. When they arrive, Don Pedro goes off for a serious chat with Leonato while Beatrice has fun teasing Benedick.

LEONATO   I learn in this letter that Don Pedro of Aragon comes this night to Messina.

MESSENGER   He is very near by this. He was not three leagues off when I left him.

league = *3 miles*

LEONATO   How many gentlemen have you lost in this action?   5

MESSENGER   But few of any sort, and none of name.

7 *"Only a few important people and nobody famous."*

LEONATO   A victory is twice itself when the achiever brings home full numbers. I find here that Don Pedro hath bestowed much honour on a young Florentine called Claudio.   10

8-9 *"A victory's twice as good when the winner comes home with all his men."*

bestowed = *given / placed*

Florentine = *person from Florence*

MESSENGER   Much deserved on his part and equally remembered by Don Pedro. He hath borne himself beyond the promise of his age, doing, in the figure of a lamb, the feats of a lion. He hath indeed better bettered expectation than you must expect of me to tell you how.   15

13-15 *"He did far better than you'd expect for his age. He looks like a lamb but he behaved like a lion."*

better bettered expectation = *done better than expected*

LEONATO   He hath an uncle here in Messina will be very much glad of it.

MESSENGER   I have already delivered him letters, and there appears much joy in him — even so much that joy could not show itself modest enough without a badge of bitterness.   20

20-22 *"He was so happy that to stop himself from looking big-headed he had to put on a show of sadness."*

LEONATO   Did he break out into tears?

break out = *burst*

MESSENGER   In great measure.

LEONATO   A kind overflow of kindness. There are no faces truer than those that are so washed. How much better is it to weep at joy than to joy at weeping!   25

BEATRICE   I pray you, is Signior Mountanto returned from the wars or no?

28 *"Mr. Cut-and-thrust"* — a 'mountanto' is a fencing move.

Does my head look big in this?

MESSENGER   I know none of that name, lady. There was none such in the army of any sort.   30

LEONATO   What is he that you ask for, niece?

HERO   My cousin means Signior Benedick of Padua.

MESSENGER   O, he's returned, and as pleasant as ever he was.   35

BEATRICE   He set up his bills here in Messina and challenged Cupid at the flight, and my uncle's fool, reading the challenge, subscribed for Cupid, and challenged him at the bird-bolt. I pray you, how many hath he killed and eaten in these wars? But how many hath he killed? For indeed I promised to eat all of his killing.   40

bills = *posters*

flight = *long, light arrow*

bird-bolt = *short, stumpy arrow, the kind Cupid uses in paintings*

LEONATO   Faith, niece, you tax Signior Benedick too much, but he'll be meet with you, I doubt it not.

43-44 *"You're too hard on Benedick, but I'm sure he'll match you."*

MESSENGER   He hath done good service, lady, in these wars.   45

musty victual = *stale food*

48 *"He's an enthusiastic eater."*
A trencher is a wooden platter.

betwixt = *between*

skirmish of wit = *argument / exchange*

60-65 *"He never wins. Last time we argued he ended up totally confused."*

sworn brother = *best friend*

69-71 *"He's as changeable as the style of his hats — it changes with every new design." The 'block' is the shaped mould hat-makers used to build a hat on.*

not in your books = *not in favour with you*

an = *if*

squarer = *brawler*

80-81 *"He will cling to him like a disease — he's easier to catch than the plague."*

ere = *before*

a' = *he*

hold = *remain*

90-92 *"Leonato, have you come to meet the cause of your troubles? Most people avoid cost but you go looking for it." Don Pedro's calling himself 'trouble' and 'cost' because he's going to be Leonato's guest.*

93-96 *"I've never seen trouble that looks like you before. When trouble goes it should leave comfort behind, but when you leave me sadness stays behind and happiness leaves."*

your grace = *polite way to speak to a duke*

BEATRICE   You had musty victual, and he hath help to eat it: he is a very valiant trencherman — he hath an excellent stomach.

MESSENGER   And a good soldier too, lady.   50

BEATRICE   And a good soldier to a lady — but what is he to a lord?

MESSENGER   A lord to a lord, a man to a man; stuffed with all honourable virtues.

BEATRICE   It is so, indeed, he is no less than a stuffed man, but for the stuffing — well, we are all mortal.   55

LEONATO   You must not, sir, mistake my niece. There is a kind of merry war betwixt Signior Benedick and her: they never meet but there's a skirmish of wit between them.

BEATRICE   Alas, he gets nothing by that. In our last conflict four of his five wits went halting off, and now is the whole man governed with one, so that if he have wit enough to keep himself warm, let him bear it for a difference between himself and his horse, for it is all the wealth that he hath left, to be known a reasonable creature. Who is his companion now? He hath every month a new sworn brother.   60   65

MESSENGER   Is't possible?

BEATRICE   Very easily possible. He wears his faith but as the fashion of his hat — it ever changes with the next block.   70

MESSENGER   I see, lady, the gentleman is not in your books.

BEATRICE   No — an he were, I would burn my study. But, I pray you, who is his companion? Is there no young squarer now that will make a voyage with him to the devil?   75

MESSENGER   He is most in the company of the right noble Claudio.

BEATRICE   O Lord, he will hang upon him like a disease — he is sooner caught than the pestilence, and the taker runs presently mad. God help the noble Claudio! If he have caught the Benedick, it will cost him a thousand pound ere a' be cured.   80

MESSENGER   I will hold friends with you, lady.   85

BEATRICE   Do, good friend.

LEONATO   You will never run mad, niece.

BEATRICE   No, not till a hot January.

MESSENGER   Don Pedro is approached.

Enter DON PEDRO, DON JOHN, CLAUDIO,
BENEDICK and BALTHASAR

DON PEDRO   Good Signior Leonato, are you come to meet your trouble? The fashion of the world is to avoid cost, and you encounter it.   90

LEONATO   Never came trouble to my house in the likeness of your grace, for trouble being gone, comfort should

---

Act 1, Scene 1

remain; but when you depart from me, sorrow abides and happiness takes his leave. 95

DON PEDRO You embrace your charge too willingly. I think this is your daughter.

LEONATO Her mother hath many times told me so.

BENEDICK Were you in doubt, sir, that you asked her? 100

LEONATO Signior Benedick, no, for then were you a child.

DON PEDRO You have it full, Benedick. We may guess by this what you are, being a man. Truly, the lady fathers herself. Be happy, lady, for you are like an honourable father. 105

BENEDICK If Signior Leonato be her father, she would not have his head on her shoulders for all Messina, as like him as she is.

BEATRICE I wonder that you will still be talking, Signior Benedick. Nobody marks you. 110

BENEDICK What, my dear Lady Disdain — are you yet living?

BEATRICE Is it possible disdain should die while she hath such meet food to feed it as Signior Benedick? Courtesy itself must convert to disdain, if you come in her presence. 115

BENEDICK Then is courtesy a turncoat. But it is certain I am loved of all ladies — only you excepted — and I would I could find in my heart that I had not a hard heart, for, truly, I love none. 120

BEATRICE A dear happiness to women, they would else have been troubled with a pernicious suitor. I thank God and my cold blood, I am of your humour for that — I had rather hear my dog bark at a crow than a man swear he loves me. 125

BENEDICK God keep your ladyship still in that mind so some gentleman or other shall scape a predestinate scratched face.

BEATRICE Scratching could not make it worse, an 'twere such a face as yours were. 130

BENEDICK Well, you are a rare parrot-teacher.

BEATRICE A bird of my tongue is better than a beast of yours.

BENEDICK I would my horse had the speed of your tongue, and so good a continuer. But keep your way, i' God's name — I have done. 135

BEATRICE You always end with a jade's trick. I know you of old.

DON PEDRO That is the sum of all, Leonato. *(turning to the others)* Signior Claudio and Signior Benedick, my dear friend Leonato hath invited you all. I tell him we shall stay here at the least a month, and he heartily prays some occasion may detain us longer. I dare swear he is no hypocrite, but prays from his heart. 140

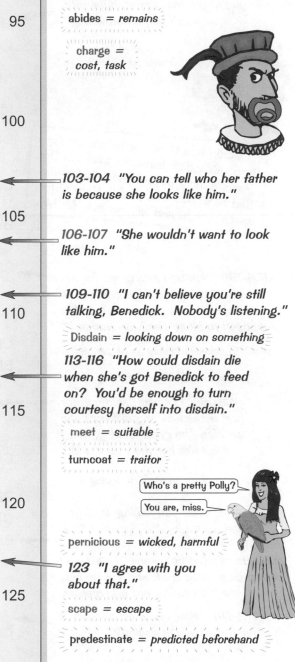

abides = *remains*

charge = *cost, task*

103-104 *"You can tell who her father is because she looks like him."*

106-107 *"She wouldn't want to look like him."*

109-110 *"I can't believe you're still talking, Benedick. Nobody's listening."*

Disdain = *looking down on something*

113-116 *"How could disdain die when she's got Benedick to feed on? You'd be enough to turn courtesy herself into disdain."*

meet = *suitable*

turncoat = *traitor*

Who's a pretty Polly?

You are, miss.

pernicious = *wicked, harmful*

123 *"I agree with you about that."*

scape = *escape*

predestinate = *predicted beforehand*

131 *In other words, she goes on and on, like someone repeating a phrase for a parrot to learn.*

132-133 *"A bird that talks like me is better than a beast that talks like you."* Beasts are 'dumb' so she's saying Benedick can't speak at all.

134-135 *"I wish my horse was as fast as you and had your stamina."*

jade = *mare*

detain = *keep*

Act 1, Scene 1

145 *"If you swear that I'm no hypocrite, you won't be proved wrong."*

reconciled to = *made peace with*

Claudio tells Benedick he's fallen for Hero. Benedick takes the mickey. Don Pedro's more helpful and tells Claudio that he'll have a word with Hero at the dance tonight and win her over for him.

note = *notice*

156-159 *"Are you asking me for my real opinion, or the one you're expecting me to give, seeing as I'm supposed to be so harsh on women?"*

speak in sober judgment = *be serious*

i'faith = *honestly*

163-165 *"I'll say this much for her: if she was any different she wouldn't be good-looking, and I don't like her the way she is."*

in sport = *joking*

170-173 *"Are you saying what you mean, or saying the opposite?"* A 'flouting jack' is someone who says the opposite of what he means. Cupid was known as a lousy shot, and Vulcan was a blacksmith, not a carpenter.

173-174 *"How are we supposed to take what you're saying?"*

her cousin = *Beatrice*

contrary = *opposite*

184-185 *"Is there not one man left in the world who isn't married?"* Elizabethans liked to joke that men with unfaithful wives could be spotted by the horns growing from their heads. Married men wear their caps 'with suspicion' because they might be hiding horns underneath.

three-score = *sixty*

187-188 *"If you want to get married and give up all your fun and freedom."*

yoke = *heavy wooden harness*

LEONATO If you swear, my lord, you shall not be forsworn. *(to Don John)* Let me bid you welcome, my lord, being reconciled to the Prince your brother. I owe you all duty. 145

DON JOHN I thank you. I am not of many words, but I thank you.

LEONATO Please it your grace lead on? 150

DON PEDRO Your hand, Leonato — we will go together.

Exeunt all except BENEDICK *and* CLAUDIO

CLAUDIO Benedick, didst thou note the daughter of Signior Leonato?

BENEDICK I noted her not, but I looked on her.

CLAUDIO Is she not a modest young lady? 155

BENEDICK Do you question me, as an honest man should do, for my simple true judgment, or would you have me speak after my custom, as being a professed tyrant to their sex?

CLAUDIO No, I pray thee speak in sober judgment. 160

BENEDICK Why, i' faith, methinks she's too low for a high praise, too brown for a fair praise and too little for a great praise. Only this commendation I can afford her, that were she other than she is, she were unhandsome, and being no other but as she is, I do not like her. 165

CLAUDIO Thou thinkest I am in sport: I pray thee tell me truly how thou lik'st her.

BENEDICK Would you buy her, that you inquire after her?

CLAUDIO Can the world buy such a jewel?

BENEDICK Yea, and a case to put it into. But speak you this with a sad brow, or do you play the flouting jack, to tell us Cupid is a good hare-finder and Vulcan a rare carpenter? Come, in what key shall a man take you, to go in the song? 170

CLAUDIO In mine eye she is the sweetest lady that ever I looked on. 175

BENEDICK I can see yet without spectacles and I see no such matter. There's her cousin, an' she were not possessed with a fury, exceeds her as much in beauty as the first of May doth the last of December. But I hope you have no intent to turn husband, have you? 180

CLAUDIO I would scarce trust myself, though I had sworn the contrary, if Hero would be my wife.

BENEDICK Is't come to this? In faith, hath not the world one man but he will wear his cap with suspicion? Shall I never see a bachelor of three-score again? Go to, i' faith, an thou wilt needs thrust thy neck into a yoke, wear the print of it and sigh away Sundays. Look, Don Pedro is returned to seek you. 185

Enter DON PEDRO

DON PEDRO What secret hath held you here, that you followed not to Leonato's? 190

BENEDICK I would your grace would constrain me to tell.

192 "I wish you would force me to tell you."

DON PEDRO I charge thee on thy allegiance.

193 "I order you to tell me."

BENEDICK You hear, Count Claudio. I can be secret as a dumb man. I would have you think so — but, on my allegiance, mark you this, on my allegiance — he is in love. With who? Now that is your grace's part. Mark how short his answer is — with Hero, Leonato's short daughter.   195

allegiance = loyalty

CLAUDIO If this were so, so were it uttered.   200

200 "If it's true, that's what he would say."

BENEDICK Like the old tale, my lord: 'it is not so, nor 'twas not so, but, indeed, God forbid it should be so.'

CLAUDIO If my passion change not shortly, God forbid it should be otherwise.

DON PEDRO Amen, if you love her, for the lady is very well worthy.   205

CLAUDIO You speak this to fetch me in, my lord.

207 "You're just saying that to get me to give myself away."

DON PEDRO By my troth, I speak my thought.

By my troth = I swear

CLAUDIO And, in faith, my lord, I spoke mine.

BENEDICK And, by my two faiths and troths, my lord, I spoke mine.   210

210 "on my word of honour to you both"

CLAUDIO That I love her, I feel.

DON PEDRO That she is worthy, I know.

BENEDICK That I neither feel how she should be loved nor know how she should be worthy, is the opinion that fire cannot melt out of me — I will die in it at the stake.   215

DON PEDRO Thou wast ever an obstinate heretic in the despite of beauty.

217-218 "You've always refused to acknowledge beauty."

CLAUDIO And never could maintain his part but in the force of his will.   220

219-220 "He only keeps the pretence up by will power."

BENEDICK That a woman conceived me, I thank her; that she brought me up, I likewise give her most humble thanks: but that I will have a recheat winded in my forehead, or hang my bugle in an invisible baldrick, all women shall pardon me. Because I will not do them the wrong to mistrust any, I will do myself the right to trust none: and the fine is, for the which I may go the finer, I will live a bachelor.   225

223-225 Benedick's saying he won't have anything to do with women because he doesn't want to be made a fool of if his wife sleeps with other men.

fine = result

DON PEDRO I shall see thee, ere I die, look pale with love.

BENEDICK With anger, with sickness, or with hunger, my lord, not with love: prove that ever I lose more blood with love than I will get again with drinking, pick out mine eyes with a ballad-maker's pen and hang me up at the door of a brothel-house for the sign of blind Cupid.   230

230-234 Benedick's insisting that there's no way he'll ever fall in love. If he does they can feel free to mock him.

DON PEDRO Well, if ever thou dost fall from this faith, thou wilt prove a notable argument.   235

235-236 "If you ever change your mind, you'll be a popular topic of conversation."

bottle = basket, used for archery practice

BENEDICK If I do, hang me in a bottle like a cat and shoot at me, and he that hits me, let him be clapped on the shoulder, and called Adam.

239 There was a famous archer called Adam Bell.

DON PEDRO Well, as time shall try — 'In time the savage bull doth bear the yoke.'   240

240 "time will be the test of that"

240-241 An old saying meaning that everyone can be tamed eventually.

Act 1, Scene 1

BENEDICK   The savage bull may — but if ever the sensible Benedick bear it, pluck off the bull's horns and set them in my forehead, and let me be vilely painted, and in such great letters as they write 'Here is good horse to hire' let them signify under my sign 'Here you may see Benedick the married man.'   245

CLAUDIO   If this should ever happen, thou wouldst be horn-mad.

DON PEDRO   Nay, if Cupid have not spent all his quiver in Venice, thou wilt quake for this shortly.   250

BENEDICK   I look for an earthquake too, then.

DON PEDRO   Well, you will temporize with the hours. In the meantime, good Signior Benedick, repair to Leonato's. Commend me to him and tell him I will not fail him at supper; for indeed he hath made great preparation.   255

BENEDICK   I have almost matter enough in me for such an embassage, and so I commit you —

CLAUDIO   To the tuition of God. From my house, if I had it —   260

DON PEDRO   The sixth of July. Your loving friend, Benedick.

BENEDICK   Nay, mock not, mock not. The body of your discourse is sometime guarded with fragments, and the guards are but slightly basted on neither. Ere you flout old ends any further, examine your conscience — and so I leave you.   265

Exit

CLAUDIO   My liege, your highness now may do me good.

DON PEDRO   My love is thine to teach. Teach it but how, And thou shalt see how apt it is to learn Any hard lesson that may do thee good.   270

CLAUDIO   Hath Leonato any son, my lord?

DON PEDRO   No child but Hero, she's his only heir. Dost thou affect her, Claudio?

CLAUDIO   O, my lord, When you went onward on this ended action,   275 I looked upon her with a soldier's eye, That liked, but had a rougher task in hand Than to drive liking to the name of love; But now I am returned and that war-thoughts Have left their places vacant, in their rooms   280 Come thronging soft and delicate desires, All prompting me how fair young Hero is, Saying, I liked her ere I went to wars.

DON PEDRO   Thou wilt be like a lover presently And tire the hearer with a book of words.   285 If thou dost love fair Hero, cherish it, And I will break with her and with her father, And thou shalt have her. Was't not to this end That thou began'st to twist so fine a story?

249-250 "If Cupid hasn't used up all his arrows in Venice, you'll suffer for this soon enough." Venice was famous for having large numbers of courtesans (classy prostitutes).

252-255 "Well, you'll soften up in time. For now, Benedick, go in to Leonato's house. Give him my best wishes and tell him I'll be sure to come for supper."

257-258 "I'm just about man enough to do the job."

258-262 These are all traditional letter endings, like 'yours sincerely' nowadays.

263-265 "Don't mock the way people end letters. The stuff you say is often pretty silly too."

268 "My lord, you could help me."

269-271 "My love is yours to teach. Just tell me how I can help you."

affect = love

this ended action = the war that's just finished

279-281 "I'm not interested in fighting anymore — I'm more interested in love."

287-289 "I'll break the news to Hero and her dad, and then she'll be yours. Isn't that what you were after when you started telling me your story?"

CLAUDIO How sweetly you do minister to love,　　290
That know love's grief by his complexion!
But lest my liking might too sudden seem,
I would have salved it with a longer treatise.

DON PEDRO What need the bridge much broader
　　　　　　　　　　　　　　　than the flood?

The fairest grant is the necessity.　　295
Look, what will serve is fit: 'tis once, thou lovest,
And I will fit thee with the remedy.
I know we shall have revelling to-night.
I will assume thy part in some disguise
And tell fair Hero I am Claudio,　　300
And in her bosom I'll unclasp my heart
And take her hearing prisoner with the force
And strong encounter of my amorous tale.
Then after to her father will I break,
And the conclusion is, she shall be thine.　　305
In practice let us put it presently.

Exeunt

290-293 *"You certainly know love when you see it! I thought my love for Hero might seem a bit sudden if I didn't prepare you for the news with a long introduction."*

294-297 *"Just do what you need to do: it's only once you fall in love, and I'll give you the cure."*

revelling = a party

299-306 *"I'll dress up as you and tell Hero I'm Claudio, and win her over with the strength of my words of love. Then I'll have a word with her father. And then she'll be yours. Let's do it."*

Antonio gets his wires crossed and tells Leonato he's heard a rumour that Don Pedro loves Hero and wants to marry her. Leonato's chuffed to bits and tells Antonio to go and give Hero the good news.

ACT 1 SCENE 2

A room in Leonato's house

Enter LEONATO and ANTONIO, meeting

LEONATO How now, brother! Where is my cousin, your
son? Hath he provided this music?

ANTONIO He is very busy about it. But, brother, I can tell
you strange news that you yet dreamt not of.

LEONATO Are they good?　　5

ANTONIO As the event stamps them, but they have a good
cover; they show well outward. The Prince and Count
Claudio, walking in a thick-pleached alley in mine
orchard, were thus much overheard by a man of mine —
the prince discovered to Claudio that he loved my niece　　10
your daughter and meant to acknowledge it this night in a
dance, and if he found her accordant, he meant to take
the present time by the top and instantly break with you
of it.

LEONATO Hath the fellow any wit that told you this?　　15

ANTONIO A good sharp fellow — I will send for him, and
question him yourself.

LEONATO No, no. We will hold it as a dream till it appear
itself, but I will acquaint my daughter withal, that she may
be the better prepared for an answer, if peradventure this　　20
be true. Go you and tell her of it.

Enter Antonio's son with a musician and attendants

Cousins, you know what you have to do. *(to musician)* O,
I cry you mercy, friend, go you with me, and I will use
your skill. Good cousin, have a care this busy time.

Exeunt

6-7 *"We'll see how things turns out in the end, but they look good on the surface."*

thick-pleached alley = a path shaded by branches

discovered = admitted

12-14 *"if she agreed, he would act on the spur of the moment and tell you all about it immediately."*

15 *"Was he a sensible fellow that told you this?"*

18-21 *"No. We'll just believe in it like a dream until it actually happens, but I'll let my daughter know, so she'll be ready to answer Don Pedro, if it really is true. You go and talk to her."*

Claudio loves Hero!

Don Pedro loves Hero!

Don John's in a bad mood about losing the war and having to suck up to his brother. Borachio tells him he's heard Claudio wants to marry Hero. Don John decides to spoil things for Claudio to cheer himself up.

ACT 1   SCENE 3
A room in Leonato's house
Enter DON JOHN *and* CONRADE

1-2 "What's up, my lord? Why are you so sad?"

CONRADE   What the goodyear, my lord? Why are you thus out of measure sad?

3-4 "There's no good reason for me to be sad, so my sadness has no limits."

DON JOHN   There is no measure in the occasion that breeds, therefore the sadness is without limit.

CONRADE   You should hear reason.   5

DON JOHN   And when I have heard it, what blessing brings it?

8-9 "If it won't make you happier, at least it will make your sadness easier to put up with."

CONRADE   If not a present remedy, at least a patient sufferance.

10-12 "I think it's a bit odd that someone as miserable as you is trying to cheer me up."

DON JOHN   I wonder that thou, being, as thou sayest thou   10 art, born under Saturn, goest about to apply a moral medicine to a mortifying mischief. I cannot hide what I am — I must be sad when I have cause and smile at no man's jests, eat when I have stomach and wait for no   15 man's leisure, sleep when I am drowsy and tend on no man's business, laugh when I am merry and claw no man in his humour.

claw = *flatter*

CONRADE   Yea, but you must not make the full show of this till you may do it without controlment. You have of late stood out against your brother, and he hath ta'en   20 you newly into his grace, where it is impossible you should take true root but by the fair weather that you make yourself — it is needful that you frame the season for your own harvest.

18-24 "You'll have to hide your true feelings until you're free to reveal them. You've only just got over this latest quarrel with your brother and you won't get properly back into his good books unless you act pleasantly. Behave yourself now and you'll reap the benefits later."

25-27 "I'd rather be a wild rose in a hedge than Don Pedro's garden rose. It suits me better to be hated by everyone, than to change my behaviour to get people to like me.'"

DON JOHN   I had rather be a canker in a hedge than a rose   25 in his grace, and it better fits my blood to be disdained of all than to fashion a carriage to rob love from any. In this, though I cannot be said to be a flattering honest man, it must not be denied but I am a plain-dealing villain. I am trusted with a muzzle and enfranchised with   30 a clog; therefore I have decreed not to sing in my cage. If I had my mouth, I would bite; if I had my liberty, I would do my liking. In the meantime let me be that I am and seek not to alter me.

30-31 "I'm trusted — but only so far..."

decreed = *decided*

discontent = *misery*

CONRADE   Can you make no use of your discontent?   35

DON JOHN   I make all use of it, for I use it only. Who comes here?

Enter BORACHIO

What news, Borachio?

BORACHIO   I came yonder from a great supper. The prince your brother is royally entertained by Leonato, and I can   40 give you intelligence of an intended marriage.

42-44 "Do you think it will give me a chance to cause some trouble? Who's the fool who's giving up a quiet life?"

DON JOHN   Will it serve for any model to build mischief on? What is he for a fool that betroths himself to unquietness?

marry = *why*

BORACHIO   Marry, it is your brother's right hand.   45

DON JOHN   Who, the most exquisite Claudio?

BORACHIO   Even he.

DON JOHN   A proper squire! And who, and who? Which way looks he?

BORACHIO   Marry, on Hero, the daughter and heir of Leonato.   50

DON JOHN   A very forward March-chick! How came you to this?   ⟵   *52 "Cheeky little monkey!"*

BORACHIO   Being entertained for a perfumer, as I was smoking a musty room, comes me the prince and   55   *54-59 "I was doing a perfumer's job, when Don Pedro came in with Claudio, having a serious conversation. I heard them agree that Don Pedro would do the courting, but then hand Hero over to Claudio."*
Claudio, hand in hand in sad conference. I whipt me behind the arras, and there heard it agreed upon that the prince should woo Hero for himself, and having obtained her, give her to Count Claudio.

DON JOHN   Come, come, let us thither. This may prove   60   *let us thither = let's go there*
food to my displeasure. That young start-up hath all the glory of my overthrow: if I can cross him any way, I bless myself every way. You are both sure, and will assist me?   ⟵   *61-63 "That young whippersnapper got all the credit for my defeat in the war. If I can do anything to annoy him, I'll be very pleased with myself."*

CONRADE   To the death, my lord.

DON JOHN   Let us to the great supper — their cheer is the   65   *65-67 "Let's go in to the big meal — they're all the happier because I've been defeated. I wish the cook felt the same way as me! Shall we go and see what we can do?"*
greater that I am subdued. Would the cook were of my mind! Shall we go prove what's to be done?

BORACHIO   We'll wait upon your lordship.

Exeunt

Act 1 — Revision Summary

These questions are all about Act 1. Some of them are to check you know what happens, some check if you understand tricky bits of language, and some of them even ask you to quote bits of the play. All this is not aimed at making your life even more of a living hell than it is already (though it probably will — sorry about that). What it is meant to do is give you the chance to test how much of the Act has sunk into that grey fuzzy place between your ears. Shoulders to the wheel, pull up your socks, tighten your belts, what ho! and good luck chaps — here we go...

SCENE 1

1) Who was the recent war between? Who won?

2) What town is Much Ado About Nothing set in?

3) Which character comes from Florence?

4) Write down a phrase from lines 57-59 to describe Beatrice's relationship with Benedick.

5) Who is Benedick's current best mate?

6) In lines 90-92, why does Don Pedro call himself "trouble"?

7) In lines 111-112, what does Benedick call Beatrice?

8) Who says, "I had rather hear my dog bark at a crow than a man swear he loves me"?

9) How long are Don Pedro and the others planning to stay at Leonato's house?

10) Why don't Benedick and Claudio go into the house with the others?

11) According to Benedick, who is "too low for a high praise, too brown for a fair praise and too little for a great praise"?

12) Also according to Benedick, who "exceeds her as much in beauty as the first of May doth the last of December"?

13) What does Don Pedro think of the girl Claudio's in love with?

14) Claudio thinks Don Pedro's just humouring him. Write down the line that tells you this.

15) Is Benedick planning on getting married in the near future?

16) Why would Cupid use up all his arrows in Venice?

17) Write down three phrases that you could use to end a letter (if you happened to be time-travelling to ye olde Elizabethan days...).

18) Write out Claudio's speech at lines 274-283 in your own words.

19) What does Don Pedro promise to do for Claudio?

20) What's "revelling"?

SCENE 2

21) Describe what a "thick-pleached alley" would look like.

22) Antonio's got the wrong end of the stick — who does he think is in love with Hero?

23) Is Leonato pleased that Hero's got an admirer?

SCENE 3

24) Who's in a grumpy sulk?

25) Who tries to cheer him up?

26) What news does Borachio bring?

27) Why does this cheer the grumpy character up?

28) Who is the "very forward March-chick"?

ACT 2   SCENE 1
A hall in Leonato's house

Enter LEONATO, ANTONIO, HERO, BEATRICE *and others*

LEONATO   Was not Count John here at supper?

ANTONIO   I saw him not.

BEATRICE   How tartly that gentleman looks! I never can see him but I am heart-burned an hour after.

HERO   He is of a very melancholy disposition.　　　5

BEATRICE   He were an excellent man that were made just in the midway between him and Benedick. The one is too like an image and says nothing, and the other too like my lady's eldest son, evermore tattling.

LEONATO   Then half Signior Benedick's tongue in Count　　10
John's mouth, and half Count John's melancholy in Signior Benedick's face —

BEATRICE   With a good leg and a good foot, uncle, and money enough in his purse — such a man would win any woman in the world, if a' could get her good-will.　　15

LEONATO   By my troth, niece, thou wilt never get thee a husband, if thou be so shrewd of thy tongue.

ANTONIO   In faith, she's too curst.

BEATRICE   Too curst is more than curst. I shall lessen God's sending that way, for it is said, 'God sends a curst　　20
cow short horns' but to a cow too curst he sends none.

LEONATO   So, by being too curst, God will send you no horns.

BEATRICE   Just, if he send me no husband, for the which blessing I am at him upon my knees every morning and　　25
evening. Lord, I could not endure a husband with a beard on his face — I had rather lie in the woollen.

LEONATO   You may light on a husband that hath no beard.

BEATRICE   What should I do with him? Dress him in my apparel and make him my waiting-gentlewoman? He　　30
that hath a beard is more than a youth, and he that hath no beard is less than a man; and he that is more than a youth is not for me, and he that is less than a man, I am not for him. Therefore, I will even take sixpence in earnest of the bearward, and lead his apes into hell.　　35

LEONATO   Well, then, go you into hell?

BEATRICE   No, but to the gate — and there will the devil meet me, like an old cuckold, with horns on his head, and say 'Get you to heaven, Beatrice, get you to heaven. Here's no place for you maids.' So deliver I up　　40
my apes, and away to Saint Peter for the heavens. He shows me where the bachelors sit, and there live we as merry as the day is long.

ANTONIO *(to Hero)*   Well, niece, I trust you will be ruled by your father.　　45

At the dance, Don Pedro gets Hero in the mood for love, Beatrice annoys Benedick and Don John tells Claudio that Don Pedro wants Hero for himself. Don Pedro explains it's not true and Hero agrees to marry Claudio. Don Pedro announces a plot to get Beatrice and Benedick together.

tartly = *sour-faced*

5 "He's always miserable."

in the midway = *halfway*

9 "Like a spoilt eldest son, always prattling away."

a' = he

16-17 "Honestly Beatrice, you'll never find a husband if you make such cutting comments."

curst = *grumpy*

19-21 She's saying that God limits the power of bad things to do harm. So a bad-tempered cow will be given short horns so that it can't do much harm. A really vicious cow wouldn't be given horns at all.

24-26 "Fair enough, so long as he doesn't send me a husband, a blessing I pray for every morning and evening."

lie in the woollen = *sleep in itchy woollen sheets*

light on = *happen to find*

apparel = *clothes*

34-35 Leading apes around hell was the supposed punishment for unmarried women. Beatrice is saying that she may as well get used to being single.

maids = *unmarried women, virgins*

40-41 "So I'll hand over my apes and go up to Saint Peter in heaven."

Act 2, Scene 1

46-49 "It's Hero's duty to agree with what her father says. But if her father suggests a husband who isn't good-looking, then Hero should please herself instead."

earth, valiant dust, wayward marl = soil, brave dust, unruly clay. In the Bible, God made the first man, Adam, from clay.

56-57 "Adam's sons are my brothers, and I believe it's a sin to marry within the family."

58-59 "If the Prince asks you to marry him, you know what to say."

61-63 "If the Prince is too hasty tell him everything comes in its own good time, and delay giving your answer."

Scotch jig = fast, energetic dance

measure = a slow, dignified dance

cinque pace = a fast, jerky dance

ancientry = old traditions

70 "You are a shrewd (and sharp-tongued) observer."

revellers = guests at the dance

Stage direction *The characters put masks on for the dance — it's a masked ball.*

favour = looks

81-82 "God forbid your face looks like that mask!"

83-84 In Roman mythology Philemon was an old man who invited Jove, the king of the gods, into his cottage for a meal.

ill-qualities = faults

BEATRICE Yes, faith. It is my cousin's duty to make curtsy and say 'Father, as it please you.' But yet for all that, cousin, let him be a handsome fellow, or else make another curtsy and say 'Father, as it please me.'

LEONATO Well, niece, I hope to see you one day fitted with a husband. 50

BEATRICE Not till God make men of some other metal than earth. Would it not grieve a woman to be overmastered with a piece of valiant dust? To make an account of her life to a clod of wayward marl? No, 55 uncle, I'll none. Adam's sons are my brethren, and, truly, I hold it a sin to match in my kindred.

LEONATO Daughter, remember what I told you — if the Prince do solicit you in that kind, you know your answer.

BEATRICE The fault will be in the music, cousin, if you be 60 not wooed in good time. If the Prince be too important, tell him there is measure in every thing and so dance out the answer. For, hear me, Hero — wooing, wedding, and repenting, is as a Scotch jig, a measure, and a cinque pace: the first suit is hot and hasty, like a Scotch jig, and 65 full as fantastical; the wedding, mannerly-modest, as a measure, full of state and ancientry; and then comes repentance and, with his bad legs, falls into the cinque pace faster and faster, till he sink into his grave.

LEONATO Cousin, you apprehend passing shrewdly. 70

BEATRICE I have a good eye, uncle — I can see a church by daylight.

LEONATO The revellers are entering, brother. Make good room.

All put on their masks

Enter DON PEDRO, CLAUDIO, BENEDICK, BALTHASAR, DON JOHN, BORACHIO, MARGARET, URSULA and others, masked

DON PEDRO Lady, will you walk about with your friend? 75

HERO So you walk softly and look sweetly and say nothing, I am yours for the walk; and especially when I walk away.

DON PEDRO With me in your company?

HERO I may say so, when I please.

DON PEDRO And when please you to say so? 80

HERO When I like your favour, for God defend the lute should be like the case!

DON PEDRO My visor is Philemon's roof — Within the house is Jove.

HERO Why, then, your visor should be thatched. 85

DON PEDRO Speak low, if you speak love.

They move aside

BALTHASAR Well, I would you did like me.

MARGARET So would not I, for your own sake, for I have many ill-qualities.

BALTHASAR Which is one? 90

MARGARET I say my prayers aloud.

BALTHASAR I love you the better — the hearers may cry
'Amen.'

MARGARET God match me with a good dancer!

BALTHASAR Amen. 95

MARGARET And God keep him out of my sight when the
dance is done! Answer, clerk.

BALTHASAR No more words — the clerk is answered.

They move aside

URSULA I know you well enough. You are Signior Antonio.

ANTONIO At a word, I am not. 100

URSULA I know you by the waggling of your head.

ANTONIO To tell you true, I counterfeit him.

URSULA You could never do him so ill-well, unless you
were the very man. Here's his dry hand up and down
— you are he, you are he. 105

ANTONIO At a word, I am not.

URSULA Come, come, do you think I do not know you by
your excellent wit? Can virtue hide itself? Go to, mum,
you are he. Graces will appear, and there's an end.

They move aside

BEATRICE Will you not tell me who told you so? 110

BENEDICK No, you shall pardon me.

BEATRICE Nor will you not tell me who you are?

BENEDICK Not now.

BEATRICE That I was disdainful, and that I had my good
wit out of the *Hundred Merry Tales* — well, this was 115
Signior Benedick that said so.

BENEDICK What's he?

BEATRICE I am sure you know him well enough.

BENEDICK Not I, believe me.

BEATRICE Did he never make you laugh? 120

BENEDICK I pray you, what is he?

BEATRICE Why, he is the Prince's jester, a very dull fool.
Only his gift is in devising impossible slanders. None
but libertines delight in him, and the commendation is
not in his wit, but in his villainy, for he both pleases men 125
and angers them, and then they laugh at him and beat
him. I am sure he is in the fleet. I would he had
boarded me.

BENEDICK When I know the gentleman, I'll tell him what
you say. 130

BEATRICE Do, do. He'll but break a comparison or two on
me, which, peradventure not marked or not laughed at,
strikes him into melancholy, and then there's a partridge
wing saved, for the fool will eat no supper that night.

Music

---

clerk = priest

counterfeit = pretend to be

103 "Do such a bad impression of him."

107-109 "Come on, do you think I can't recognise your good sense of humour? Can you hide virtue? Go on, quiet now, I know it's you. Good qualities always show through." Ursula knows it's Antonio even though he's wearing a mask.

114-116 "So I'm disdainful and I get my jokes out of the Hundred Merry Tales — I bet it was Benedick who said that."

118-119 Benedick and Beatrice are wearing masks. Benedick pretends to be someone else, so that he can hear what Beatrice says about him. But... Beatrice has already twigged that it's Benedick and has some fun insulting him.

123-128 "His only talent is coming up with ridiculous insults. Only silly people like his humour, and they don't like his jokes but his insults. He amuses some men with his insults and annoys others — he gets laughed at and beaten up. I'm sure he's in the navy. I wish he had tried it on with me."

131-133 "He'll just make a couple of jokes at my expense, and when no one notices or laughs at them, he'll fall into a sulk"

Act 2, Scene 1

14

We must follow the leaders.   135

BENEDICK   In every good thing.

BEATRICE   Nay, if they lead to any ill, I will leave them at the next turning.

Dance.

Then exeunt all except DON JOHN,
BORACHIO and CLAUDIO

139-141 "My brother is definitely keen on Hero, and has gone with Leonato to tell him about it. The ladies have all joined the dance behind Hero, and there's just one masked man standing out of the dance."

DON JOHN   Sure my brother is amorous on Hero and hath withdrawn her father to break with him about it. The ladies follow her and but one visor remains.   140

BORACHIO   And that is Claudio. I know him by his bearing.

DON JOHN   Are not you Signior Benedick?

CLAUDIO   You know me well — I am he.

145-146 Don John pretends to think that Claudio is Benedick. Don John lies and says that Don Pedro wants Hero for himself. He does this to wind Claudio up.

147 She's not good enough for him.

DON JOHN   Signior, you are very near my brother in his love; he is enamoured on Hero. I pray you, dissuade him from her; she is no equal for his birth — you may do the part of an honest man in it.   145

CLAUDIO   How know you he loves her?

DON JOHN   I heard him swear his affection.   150

BORACHIO   So did I too, and he swore he would marry her tonight.

DON JOHN   Come, let us to the banquet.

banquet = late-night pudding course

Exeunt DON JOHN *and* BORACHIO

154-164 "I answered in the name of Benedick, but I heard the bad news with Claudio's ears. Clearly Don Pedro's wooing Hero for himself. Friends are faithful, except when it comes to love. People in love should speak for themselves, not trust others, I should have known better."
Claudio falls for Don John's wind up.

CLAUDIO   Thus answer I in the name of Benedick,
But hear these ill news with the ears of Claudio.   155
'Tis certain so, the prince woos for himself.
Friendship is constant in all other things
Save in the office and affairs of love.
Therefore, all hearts in love use their own tongues,
Let every eye negotiate for itself   160
And trust no agent, for beauty is a witch
Against whose charms faith melteth into blood.
This is an accident of hourly proof,
Which I mistrusted not. Farewell, therefore, Hero!

Re-enter BENEDICK

It's all over...

BENEDICK   Count Claudio?   165

CLAUDIO   Yea, the same.

BENEDICK   Come, will you go with me?

CLAUDIO   Whither?

Whither = where

169-172 "To the next willow tree, to deal with your business, count. How will you wear your garland? Around your neck, like a money-lender's chain? Or under your arm, like a lieutenant's sash?" Willow trees were a symbol of abandoned lovers.

BENEDICK   Even to the next willow, about your own business, county. What fashion will you wear the garland of? About your neck, like an usurer's chain? Or under your arm, like a lieutenant's scarf? You must wear it one way, for the prince hath got your Hero.   170

CLAUDIO   I wish him joy of her.

drover = someone who sells cows

176-177 "Do you think the Prince would have treated you like that?" Benedick is surprised that Claudio is so quick to believe the worst.

BENEDICK   Why, that's spoken like an honest drover. So they sell bullocks. But did you think the Prince would have served you thus?   175

CLAUDIO I pray you, leave me.

BENEDICK Ho! Now you strike like the blind man! 'Twas the boy that stole your meat, and you'll beat the post. 180

CLAUDIO If it will not be, I'll leave you.

Exit

BENEDICK Alas, poor hurt fowl! Now will he creep into sedges. But that my Lady Beatrice should know me, and not know me! The Prince's fool! Ha? It may be I go under that title because I am merry. Yea, but so I am 185 apt to do myself wrong. I am not so reputed. It is the base, though bitter, disposition of Beatrice that puts the world into her person and so gives me out. Well, I'll be revenged as I may.

Re-enter DON PEDRO

DON PEDRO Now, signior, where's the count? Did you 190 see him?

BENEDICK Troth, my lord, I have played the part of Lady Fame. I found him here as melancholy as a lodge in a warren. I told him, and I think I told him true, that your grace had got the good will of this young lady, and I 195 offered him my company to a willow-tree, either to make him a garland, as being forsaken, or to bind him up a rod, as being worthy to be whipped.

DON PEDRO To be whipped! What's his fault?

BENEDICK The flat transgression of a schoolboy, who, 200 being overjoyed with finding a bird's nest, shows it his companion, and he steals it.

DON PEDRO Wilt thou make a trust a transgression? The transgression is in the stealer.

BENEDICK Yet it had not been amiss the rod had been 205 made, and the garland too. For the garland he might have worn himself, and the rod he might have bestowed on you, who, as I take it, have stolen his bird's nest.

DON PEDRO I will but teach them to sing, and restore them to the owner. 210

BENEDICK If their singing answer your saying, by my faith, you say honestly.

DON PEDRO The Lady Beatrice hath a quarrel to you. The gentleman that danced with her told her she is much wronged by you. 215

BENEDICK O, she misused me past the endurance of a block! An oak but with one green leaf on it would have answered her; my very visor began to assume life and scold with her. She told me, not thinking I had been myself, that I was the Prince's jester, that I was duller 220 than a great thaw; huddling jest upon jest with such impossible conveyance upon me that I stood like a man at a mark, with a whole army shooting at me. She speaks poniards and every word stabs. If her breath were as terrible as her terminations, there were no living 225 near her — she would infect to the north star. I would

179-180 "Don't take it out on me, it's nothing to do with me."

182-183 "hide away and sulk."

184-188 "Maybe people do call me that because I'm cheery. But I don't think I should be so hard on myself. That's not my reputation. It's Beatrice's sour nature that makes her talk as though what she thinks is what everyone thinks."

Troth = in truth, honestly

192-193 "reported on what's going on."

193-194 "as dismal as a shed at a rabbit warren." A rabbit warren was a place where rabbits were bred for eating — a fairly out of the way, dreary kind of place.

200-202 "The wrong-doing of a schoolboy, who's so happy to find a birds' nest that he shows it to his friend, who steals it."

203-204 "Are you calling honesty wrong-doing? It's the person who does the stealing who does wrong."

bestowed = used

Sing up, ladies!

213 "Beatrice has got a bone to pick with you."

216-219 "She would have tested the patience of a block! An oak tree would have been riled by her — my mask was on the verge of arguing with her."

duller than a great thaw = more boring than the spring thaw (when roads were blocked with mud and it was impossible to travel)

conveyance = speed

poniards = daggers

mark = target

terminations = words

227-228 *"even if she was as rich as Adam before he sinned and left Paradise."*

228-235 *"She would have set Hercules to work turning the meat-spit and broken up his club to feed the fire too. Don't talk about her — you'll find hellish Ate (goddess of discord) in good form. I wish some magician would conjure her up, because as long as she's here a man gets no more peace than in hell, and people even commit sins on purpose because they'd rather be in hell than here."*

disquiet = unease

perturbation = annoyance, misery

Antipodes = southern hemisphere (Australia hadn't been discovered yet)

Prester John = mythical Christian king of a country in Asia

great Cham = Great Khan, ruler of the Mongol empire

embassage = trip

harpy = bird-woman

256 *"You have upset him."*

258-259 *Beatrice deliberately misunderstands Don Pedro's phrase 'put down' as 'laid down in bed' — she doesn't want to have Benedick's children in case they turn out to be fools.*

Wherefore = why

267 *A super-funny pun on 'Seville orange'. Claudio's pretending to be polite because he's got into such a state thinking Don Pedro is wooing Hero for himself.*

complexion = colour

blazon = description

270 *"If that is what Claudio's thinking he's wrong."*

not marry her, though she were endowed with all that Adam had left him before he transgressed. She would have made Hercules have turned spit, yea, and have cleft his club to make the fire too. Come, talk not of her — you shall find her the infernal Ate in good apparel. I would to God some scholar would conjure her, for certainly, while she is here, a man may live as quiet in hell as in a sanctuary, and people sin upon purpose, because they would go thither; so, indeed, all disquiet, horror and perturbation follows her. — 230, 235

Enter CLAUDIO, BEATRICE, HERO, *and* LEONATO

DON PEDRO Look, here she comes.

BENEDICK Will your grace command me any service to the world's end? I will go on the slightest errand now to the Antipodes that you can devise to send me on. I will fetch you a tooth-picker now from the furthest inch of Asia, bring you the length of Prester John's foot, fetch you a hair off the great Cham's beard, do you any embassage to the Pygmies, rather than hold three words' conference with this harpy. You have no employment for me? — 240, 245

DON PEDRO None, but to desire your good company.

BENEDICK O God, sir, here's a dish I love not — I cannot endure my Lady Tongue.

Exit

DON PEDRO Come, lady, come, you have lost the heart of Signior Benedick. — 250

BEATRICE Indeed, my lord, he lent it me awhile, and I gave him use for it, a double heart for his single one. Marry, once before he won it of me with false dice, therefore your grace may well say I have lost it. — 255

DON PEDRO You have put him down, lady, you have put him down.

BEATRICE So I would not he should do me, my lord, lest I should prove the mother of fools. I have brought Count Claudio, whom you sent me to seek. — 260

DON PEDRO Why, how now, count! Wherefore are you sad?

CLAUDIO Not sad, my lord.

DON PEDRO How then? Sick?

CLAUDIO Neither, my lord. — 265

BEATRICE The count is neither sad, nor sick, nor merry, nor well, but civil count, civil as an orange, and something of that jealous complexion.

DON PEDRO I' faith, lady, I think your blazon to be true, though, I'll be sworn, if he be so, his conceit is false. Here, Claudio, I have wooed in thy name, and fair Hero is won. I have broke with her father, and his good will obtained. Name the day of marriage, and God give thee joy! — 270

LEONATO Count, take of me my daughter, and with her 275
my fortunes. His grace hath made the match, and all
grace say Amen to it.

BEATRICE Speak, count — 'tis your cue.

CLAUDIO Silence is the perfectest herald of joy. I were but 280
little happy, if I could say how much. Lady, as you are
mine, I am yours. I give away myself for you and dote
upon the exchange.

279-280 "Silence is the best sign of joy. I wouldn't be very happy if I could say how happy I was."

She loves me!

BEATRICE Speak, cousin, or, if you cannot, stop his
mouth with a kiss, and let not him speak neither.

DON PEDRO In faith, lady, you have a merry heart. 285

BEATRICE Yea, my lord, I thank it — poor fool, it keeps on
the windy side of care. My cousin tells him in his ear
that he is in her heart.

286-287 "it stays upwind from care", i.e. out of care's way.

CLAUDIO And so she doth, cousin.

BEATRICE Good Lord, for alliance! Thus goes every one 290
to the world but I, and I am sunburnt. I may sit in a
corner and cry heigh-ho for a husband!

290-292 Beatrice pretends to be upset that everyone's getting married apart from her.

DON PEDRO Lady Beatrice, I will get you one.

BEATRICE I would rather have one of your father's
getting. Hath your grace ne'er a brother like you? Your 295
father got excellent husbands, if a maid could come by
them.

294-295 "I would rather have one fathered by your father."

DON PEDRO Will you have me, lady?

BEATRICE No, my lord, unless I might have another for
working-days: your grace is too costly to wear every 300
day. But, I beseech your grace, pardon me — I was
born to speak all mirth and no matter.

beseech = beg

302 "just talk in jokes and never seriously."

DON PEDRO Your silence most offends me, and to be
merry best becomes you, for, out of question, you were
born in a merry hour. 305

BEATRICE No, sure, my lord, my mother cried, but then
there was a star danced, and under that was I born.
Cousins — God give you joy!

LEONATO Niece, will you look to those things I told you
of? 310

BEATRICE I cry you mercy, uncle. By your grace's
pardon.

311-312 "Forgive me, uncle. Excuse me, your grace."

Exit

DON PEDRO By my troth, a pleasant-spirited lady.

LEONATO There's little of the melancholy element in her,
my lord. She is never sad but when she sleeps, and not 315
ever sad then, for I have heard my daughter say, she
hath often dreamed of unhappiness and waked herself
with laughing.

DON PEDRO She cannot endure to hear tell of a
husband. 320

endure = bear

LEONATO O, by no means — she mocks all her wooers
out of suit.

321-322 "she makes fun of everyone who flirts with her until they give up"

DON PEDRO She were an excellent wife for Benedick.

Act 2, Scene 1

rites = customs

a just seven-night = a full week

breathing = wait, pause

Hercules = Greek hero who had to perform 12 near-impossible tasks

338-340 "I'd like to see them married, and I'm sure I can pull it off, if you three give me the help I ask for."

ten nights' watchings = ten sleepless nights

drift = plan

LEONATO   O Lord, my lord, if they were but a week married, they would talk themselves mad. 325

DON PEDRO   County Claudio, when mean you to go to church?

CLAUDIO   To-morrow, my lord — time goes on crutches till love have all his rites.

LEONATO   Not till Monday, my dear son, which is hence a just seven-night, and a time too brief, too, to have all things answer my mind. 330

DON PEDRO   Come, you shake the head at so long a breathing — but, I warrant thee, Claudio, the time shall not go dully by us. I will in the interim undertake one of Hercules' labours, which is, to bring Signior Benedick and the Lady Beatrice into a mountain of affection the one with the other. I would fain have it a match, and I doubt not but to fashion it, if you three will but minister such assistance as I shall give you direction. 335 340

LEONATO   My lord, I am for you, though it cost me ten nights' watchings.

CLAUDIO   And I, my lord.

DON PEDRO   And you too, gentle Hero?

HERO   I will do any modest office, my lord, to help my cousin to a good husband. 345

DON PEDRO   And Benedick is not the unhopefullest husband that I know. Thus far can I praise him — he is of a noble strain, of approved valour and confirmed honesty. I will teach you how to humour your cousin, that she shall fall in love with Benedick; and I, with your two helps, will so practise on Benedick that, in despite of his quick wit and his queasy stomach, he shall fall in love with Beatrice. If we can do this, Cupid is no longer an archer: his glory shall be ours, for we are the only love-gods. Go in with me, and I will tell you my drift. 350 355

Exeunt

Don John swears to put a stop to the wedding. Borachio hatches a plan to help him spoil the fun.

ACT 2 SCENE 2
A hall in Leonato's house
Enter DON JOHN *and* BORACHIO

DON JOHN   It is so — the Count Claudio shall marry the daughter of Leonato.

BORACHIO   Yea, my lord, but I can cross it.

DON JOHN   Any bar, any cross, any impediment will be medicinable to me. I am sick in displeasure to him, and whatsoever comes athwart his affection ranges evenly with mine. How canst thou cross this marriage?   5

BORACHIO   Not honestly, my lord, but so covertly that no dishonesty shall appear in me.

DON JOHN   Show me briefly how.   10

BORACHIO   I think I told your lordship a year since, how much I am in the favour of Margaret, the waiting gentlewoman to Hero.

DON JOHN   I remember.

BORACHIO   I can, at any unseasonable instant of the night, appoint her to look out at her lady's chamber window.   15

DON JOHN   What life is in that, to be the death of this marriage?

BORACHIO   The poison of that lies in you to temper. Go you to the Prince your brother; spare not to tell him that he hath wronged his honour in marrying the renowned Claudio — whose estimation do you mightily hold up — to a contaminated stale, such a one as Hero.   20

DON JOHN   What proof shall I make of that?   25

BORACHIO   Proof enough to misuse the prince, to vex Claudio, to undo Hero and kill Leonato. Look you for any other issue?

DON JOHN   Only to despite them, I will endeavour any thing.   30

BORACHIO   Go, then, find me a meet hour to draw Don Pedro and the Count Claudio alone. Tell them that you know that Hero loves me, intend a kind of zeal both to the Prince and Claudio (as in love of your brother's honour, who hath made this match, and his friend's reputation, who is thus like to be cozened with the semblance of a maid) that you have discovered thus. They will scarcely believe this without trial — offer them instances, which shall bear no less likelihood than to see me at her chamber-window, hear me call Margaret Hero, hear Margaret term me Claudio, and bring them   35   40

---

cross = *prevent*

4-7 *"Anything that gets in the way of the marriage will be good for me. I am fed up of Claudio, and whatever upsets him, suits me. How can you prevent the marriage?"*

covertly = *sneakily*

waiting gentlewoman = *servant*

15-17 *"I can get her to look out of the window of Hero's room at any time of night, no matter how late."*

20-24 *"It will be up to you to turn it to your own evil ends. Go to Don Pedro. Tell him that his own reputation is threatened by encouraging Claudio — who you think is a marvellous chap — to marry a dirty old slapper like Hero."*

25 *"How can I prove that?"*

issue = *result*   misuse = *deceive*

29-30 *"I'll try anything to spite that lot."*

31-37 *"Find a suitable time to talk to Don Pedro and Claudio alone. Tell them that you know Hero loves me, pretend to be really upset for the prince and Claudio that you've found this out (for Don Pedro because his reputation's at risk, as the man who set the marriage up, and for Claudio, because he's likely to be fooled by someone who only seems to be a virgin)."*

instances = *proof*

43-46 "In the meantime, I'll make sure Hero's elsewhere, and it will seem so certain that Hero is disloyal that jealousy will take the place of evidence, and all the wedding plans will be cancelled."

47-49 "I don't care what the results will be, I'm going to see this through. Make this plan work and I'll give you a thousand ducats."

50-51 "You stick to the story we've agreed and I won't let you down."

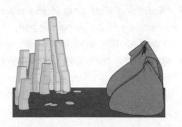

to see this the very night before the intended wedding. For in the meantime I will so fashion the matter that Hero shall be absent, and there shall appear such seeming truth of Hero's disloyalty that jealousy shall be called assurance and all the preparation overthrown. 45

DON JOHN Grow this to what adverse issue it can, I will put it in practice. Be cunning in the working this, and thy fee is a thousand ducats.

BORACHIO Be you constant in the accusation, and my 50 cunning shall not shame me.

DON JOHN I will presently go learn their day of marriage.

Exeunt

ACT 2 SCENE 3
Leonato's orchard

Enter BENEDICK

Benedick's hanging around in the garden. He thinks Claudio's a fool for falling in love. Don Pedro, Claudio and Leonato go on about how Beatrice is in love with Benedick, knowing that Benedick is listening in to their conversation. He falls straight into their trap...

BENEDICK   Boy!

Enter BOY

BOY   Signior?

BENEDICK   In my chamber-window lies a book — bring it hither to me in the orchard.

BOY   I am here already, sir.   5

BENEDICK   I know that, but I would have thee hence, and here again.

Exit BOY

hither = *here*

hence = *away from here*

I do much wonder that one man — seeing how much another man is a fool when he dedicates his behaviours to love — will, after he hath laughed at such   10
shallow follies in others, become the argument of his own scorn by falling in love; and such a man is Claudio. I have known when there was no music with him but the drum and the fife, and now had he rather hear the tabor and the pipe. I have known when he would have walked   15
ten mile a-foot to see a good armour; and now will he lie ten nights awake, carving the fashion of a new doublet. He was wont to speak plain and to the purpose, like an honest man and a soldier; and now is he turned orthography — his words are a very fantastical banquet,   20
just so many strange dishes. May I be so converted and see with these eyes? I cannot tell — I think not — I will not be sworn, but love may transform me to an oyster; but I'll take my oath on it, till he have made an oyster of me, he shall never make me such a fool. One woman   25
is fair, yet I am well; another is wise, yet I am well; another virtuous, yet I am well; but till all graces be in one woman, one woman shall not come in my grace. Rich she shall be, that's certain; wise, or I'll none; virtuous, or I'll never cheapen her; fair, or I'll never look   30
on her; mild, or come not near me; noble, or not I for an angel; of good discourse, an excellent musician, and her hair shall be of what colour it please God. Ha! The Prince and Monsieur Love! I will hide me in the arbour.

Withdraws

Enter DON PEDRO, CLAUDIO, *and* LEONATO

DON PEDRO   Come, shall we hear this music?   35

CLAUDIO   Yea, my good lord. How still the evening is,
As hushed on purpose to grace harmony!

DON PEDRO   See you where Benedick hath hid himself?

CLAUDIO   O, very well, my lord. The music ended,
We'll fit the kid-fox with a pennyworth.   40

Enter BALTHASAR, *with music*

8-12 *"I think it's amazing how a man — who has seen how foolish another man makes himself when he gets obsessed about love — will become the exact thing he once criticised and fall in love himself — and that's the kind of man Claudio is."*

13-15 *"I remember when he only had ears for military music, now it's all namby-pamby ceremonial music."*

a-foot = *on foot*

doublet = *fancy jacket*

18-25 *"He used to speak plainly and clearly, like an honest man and a soldier — now he talks in a flowery style. Could I be transformed and end up like him? I don't know — I don't think so — I couldn't swear to it, but love could turn me into an oyster, but I will make an oath that until love does turn me into an oyster, he won't make such a fool out of me."*

27-28 *"Until one woman combines all good qualities, not one woman will come into my good books."*

discourse = *conversation*

arbour = *shady garden nook*

36-37 *"What a calm evening, as though it had gone quiet on purpose to make the music sound better."*

39-40 *"When the music's over we'll set the fox up for a dodgy deal." i.e. they're going to play a trick on Benedick.*

42-43 "My good lord, don't demand my bad voice to spoil the music more than once."

44-46 "It's still the mark of excellence to deny it. Go on, sing, and let me stop wooing you."

48-50 "Many wooers start off thinking the woman they're wooing isn't worth it, but they still woo, and they still swear they're in love."

51-52 "If you want to carry on arguing, at least do it in a song."

crotchets = musical notes, but also silly things

56-58 "Isn't it odd that instruments made of sheep's insides can express such strong feelings."

blithe = happy

bonny = good looking

shift = emergency

80-84 "If a dog had howled like that they would have hanged him, and I pray to God that his bad voice isn't an evil omen. I would rather have heard a night-raven, whatever plague came after."

lief = gladly

DON PEDRO Come, Balthasar, we'll hear that song again.

BALTHASAR O, good my lord, tax not so bad a voice
 To slander music any more than once.

DON PEDRO It is the witness still of excellency
 To put a strange face on his own perfection.   45
 I pray thee, sing, and let me woo no more.

BALTHASAR Because you talk of wooing, I will sing,
 Since many a wooer doth commence his suit
 To her he thinks not worthy, yet he woos,
 Yet will he swear he loves.

DON PEDRO   Now, pray thee, come;   50
 Or, if thou wilt hold longer argument,
 Do it in notes.

BALTHASAR   Note this before my notes;
 There's not a note of mine that's worth the noting.

DON PEDRO Why, these are very crotchets that he
                                                  speaks —
 Note, notes, forsooth, and nothing.   55

Music

BENEDICK Now, divine air! Now is his soul ravished! Is it
 not strange that sheep's guts should hale souls out of
 men's bodies? Well, a horn for my money, when all's
 done.

BALTHASAR *(sings) Sigh no more, ladies, sigh no more,*   60
    Men were deceivers ever,
    One foot in sea and one on shore,
    To one thing constant never;
    Then sigh not so, but let them go,
    And be you blithe and bonny,   65
    Converting all your sounds of woe
    Into hey nonny, nonny.

    Sing no more ditties, sing no moe,
    Of dumps so dull and heavy.
    The fraud of men was ever so,   70
    Since summer first was leavy;
    Then sigh not so, but let them go,
    And be you blithe and bonny,
    Converting all your sounds of woe
    Into hey nonny, nonny.   75

DON PEDRO By my troth, a good song.

BALTHASAR And an ill singer, my lord.

DON PEDRO Ha! No, no, faith! Thou singest well enough
 for a shift.

BENEDICK An he had been a dog that should have   80
 howled thus, they would have hanged him, and I pray
 God his bad voice bode no mischief. I had as lief have
 heard the night-raven, come what plague could have
 come after it.

DON PEDRO   Yea, marry, dost thou hear, Balthasar? I pray   85
thee, get us some excellent music, for to-morrow night
we would have it at the Lady Hero's chamber-window.

BALTHASAR   The best I can, my lord.

DON PEDRO   Do so. Farewell.

Exit BALTHASAR

Come hither, Leonato. What was it you told me of today,   90
that your niece Beatrice was in love with Signior
Benedick?

CLAUDIO   O ay, stalk on, stalk on — the fowl sits. I did
never think that lady would have loved any man.

LEONATO   No, nor I neither, but most wonderful that she   95
should so dote on Signior Benedick, whom she hath in
all outward behaviours seemed ever to abhor.

BENEDICK   Is't possible? Sits the wind in that corner?

LEONATO   By my troth, my lord, I cannot tell what to think
of it but that she loves him with an enraged affection —   100
it is past the infinite of thought.

DON PEDRO   May be she doth but counterfeit.

CLAUDIO   Faith, like enough.

LEONATO   O God, counterfeit! There was never counterfeit
of passion came so near the life of passion as she   105
discovers it.

DON PEDRO   Why, what effects of passion shows she?

CLAUDIO   Bait the hook well — this fish will bite.

LEONATO   What effects, my lord? She will sit you, you
heard my daughter tell you how.   110

CLAUDIO   She did, indeed.

DON PEDRO   How, how, pray you? You amaze me. I
would have thought her spirit had been invincible against
all assaults of affection.

LEONATO   I would have sworn it had, my lord, especially   115
against Benedick.

BENEDICK   I should think this a gull, but that the white-
bearded fellow speaks it. Knavery cannot, sure, hide
himself in such reverence.

CLAUDIO   He hath ta'en the infection. Hold it up.   120

DON PEDRO   Hath she made her affection known to
Benedick?

LEONATO   No, and swears she never will. That's her
torment.

CLAUDIO   'Tis true, indeed, so your daughter says. "Shall   125
I," says she, "that have so oft encountered him with
scorn, write to him that I love him?"

LEONATO   This says she now when she is beginning to
write to him, for she'll be up twenty times a night, and
there will she sit in her smock till she have writ a sheet   130
of paper — my daughter tells us all.

marry = truly

93 "Benedick is listening, ready to fall into the trap."

95-97 "No, me neither, but it's amazing that she should be so mad about Benedick, who she always seemed to detest."

98 "Is it possible? Is that the way things are?"

101 "it's beyond all understanding"

102 "Maybe she's just pretending."

104-106 "No one can pretend as well as that."

gull = trick

118-119 "Mischief can't be concealed behind such a dignified appearance"

120 "Benedick has fallen for the trick."

encountered = treated

Act 2, Scene 3

138-142 *"Oh, she tore the letter into a thousand little bits, told herself off for being so shameless as to write to him when she knew he would reject her. 'I'm judging him,' she says 'by my own standards, because I'd turn him down if he wrote to me, even though I love him'."*

147-149 *"the strength of her feelings has overpowered her so much that my daughter is sometimes afraid she might even kill herself."*

discover = reveal

152-153 *"What would be the point? He'd just make a big joke out of it and make her suffering worse."*

154 *"If he did, it would be best to hang him."*

159-161 *"Oh, my lord, when wisdom and passion compete in such a tender body, it's ten to one that passion will succeed."*

163-165 *"I wish it was me she had given her heart to: I would have set aside all other considerations and married her."*

a' = he

ere = before

170-172 *"if he does woo her, she'll die rather than hold back one breath of her usual crossness"*

173-175 *"It's the best plan. If she did offer him her love, it's more than likely he'd turn her down, because, as you all know, he's dreadfully mean-spirited."*

177 *"He puts on a good show of cheerfulness."*

CLAUDIO Now you talk of a sheet of paper, I remember a pretty jest your daughter told us of.

LEONATO O — when she had writ it and was reading it over, she found Benedick and Beatrice between the sheet? — 135

CLAUDIO That.

LEONATO O, she tore the letter into a thousand halfpence, railed at herself, that she should be so immodest to write to one that she knew would flout her. "I measure him," says she, "by my own spirit, for I should flout him, if he writ to me, yea, though I love him, I should." — 140

CLAUDIO Then down upon her knees she falls, weeps, sobs, beats her heart, tears her hair, prays, curses, "O sweet Benedick! God give me patience!" — 145

LEONATO She doth indeed. My daughter says so, and the ecstasy hath so much overborne her that my daughter is sometime afeared she will do a desperate outrage to herself. It is very true.

DON PEDRO It were good that Benedick knew of it by some other, if she will not discover it. — 150

CLAUDIO To what end? He would make but a sport of it and torment the poor lady worse.

DON PEDRO An he should, it were an alms to hang him. She's an excellent sweet lady, and, out of all suspicion, she is virtuous. — 155

CLAUDIO And she is exceeding wise.

DON PEDRO In every thing but in loving Benedick.

LEONATO O, my lord, wisdom and blood combatting in so tender a body, we have ten proofs to one that blood hath the victory. I am sorry for her, as I have just cause, being her uncle and her guardian. — 160

DON PEDRO I would she had bestowed this dotage on me: I would have daffed all other respects and made her half myself. I pray you, tell Benedick of it, and hear what a' will say. — 165

LEONATO Were it good, think you?

CLAUDIO Hero thinks surely she will die, for she says she will die, if he love her not, and she will die, ere she make her love known, and she will die, if he woo her, rather than she will bate one breath of her accustomed crossness. — 170

DON PEDRO She doth well. If she should make tender of her love, 'tis very possible he'll scorn it, for the man, as you know all, hath a contemptible spirit. — 175

CLAUDIO He is a very proper man.

DON PEDRO He hath indeed a good outward happiness.

CLAUDIO Before God! — and, in my mind, very wise.

DON PEDRO He doth indeed show some sparks that are like wit. — 180

CLAUDIO And I take him to be valiant.

DON PEDRO   As Hector, I assure you, and in the managing of quarrels you may say he is wise, for either he avoids them with great discretion, or undertakes them with a most Christian-like fear.   185

LEONATO   If he do fear God, a' must necessarily keep peace: if he break the peace, he ought to enter into a quarrel with fear and trembling.

DON PEDRO   And so will he do, for the man doth fear God, howsoever it seems not in him by some large jests he will make. Well, I am sorry for your niece. Shall we go seek Benedick, and tell him of her love?   190

CLAUDIO   Never tell him, my lord. Let her wear it out with good counsel.

LEONATO   Nay, that's impossible — she may wear her heart out first.   195

DON PEDRO   Well, we will hear further of it by your daughter. Let it cool the while. I love Benedick well, and I could wish he would modestly examine himself, to see how much he is unworthy so good a lady.   200

LEONATO   My lord, will you walk? Dinner is ready.

CLAUDIO *(Aside)*   If he do not dote on her upon this, I will never trust my expectation.

DON PEDRO *(Aside)*   Let there be the same net spread for her, and that must your daughter and her gentlewomen carry. The sport will be when they hold one an opinion of another's dotage, and no such matter. That's the scene that I would see, which will be merely a dumb-show. Let us send her to call him in to dinner.   205

Exeunt DON PEDRO, CLAUDIO *and* LEONATO

BENEDICK *(coming forward)*   This can be no trick. The conference was sadly borne. They have the truth of this from Hero. They seem to pity the lady: it seems her affections have their full bent. Love me! Why, it must be requited. I hear how I am censured. They say I will bear myself proudly, if I perceive the love come from her. They say too that she will rather die than give any sign of affection. I did never think to marry. I must not seem proud: happy are they that hear their detractions and can put them to mending. They say the lady is fair — 'tis a truth, I can bear them witness; and virtuous — 'tis so, I cannot reprove it; and wise, but for loving me — by my troth, it is no addition to her wit, nor no great argument of her folly, for I will be horribly in love with her. I may chance have some odd quirks and remnants of wit broken on me, because I have railed so long against marriage, but doth not the appetite alter? A man loves the meat in his youth that he cannot endure in his age. Shall quips and sentences and these paper bullets of the brain awe a man from the career of his humour? No, the world must be peopled. When I said I would die a bachelor, I did not think I should live till I were married.   210   215   220   225   230

Hector = hero on the Trojan side in the Trojan War, known for his courage

183-184 "he takes great care to avoid them"

Harrumph!

193-194 "Let her get over it by thinking it all through."

197-200 "Well, we'll hear more from Hero. Let things calm down in the meantime. I really like Benedick, and I wish he'd take a good look at himself and realise he doesn't deserve such a good lady."

202-203 "If he hasn't fallen for her now, I'll never trust my judgement again."

204-209 "The same trap must be set for Beatrice, and your daughter and her servants must do it. The fun will start when they both believe the other one's in love with them. That's the scene I want to see, it'll be no more than a puppet show."

210-211 "The conversation was too serious."

have their full bent = are in full flow

213-215 "she must have my love in return. I heard their criticisms. They say I'll be all proud, if I see that she loves me."

218-219 "it's a good thing to take criticism on board."

fair = beautiful

reprove = contradict

223-226 "People will tease me and make jokes about me, because I've criticised marriage for so long, but don't tastes change?"

228-229 "Should gags and wisecracks be allowed to scare a man away from what he really wants to do?"

marks = signs

 ouch

241-243 *"About as much pleasure as you can fit on a knife point, and choke a jackdaw with. You're not hungry."*

244-248 *Benedick thinks that Beatrice is dropping hints about being in love with him.*

Jew = *in Elizabethan times it was a common prejudice that Jews were selfish and not to be trusted*

Here comes Beatrice. By this day she's a fair lady! I do spy some marks of love in her.

Enter BEATRICE

BEATRICE   Against my will I am sent to bid you come in to dinner. 235

BENEDICK   Fair Beatrice, I thank you for your pains.

BEATRICE   I took no more pains for those thanks than you take pains to thank me. If it had been painful, I would not have come.

BENEDICK   You take pleasure then in the message? 240

BEATRICE   Yea, just so much as you may take upon a knife's point and choke a daw withal. You have no stomach, signior. Fare you well.

Exit

BENEDICK   Ha! "Against my will I am sent to bid you come in to dinner," — there's a double meaning in that. "I took 245 no more pains for those thanks than you took pains to thank me," — that's as much as to say, "Any pains that I take for you is as easy as thanks." If I do not take pity of her, I am a villain; if I do not love her, I am a Jew. I will go get her picture. 250

Exit

Act 2 — Revision Summary

Well the plot's thickening up... but is it getting any easier to understand? Probably not, if I know my Shakespeare. Work your way through these questions, and if they seem a bit tricky at first, don't give up — keep going. Working out the answers to each question will help you understand the whole act better. And that's what we all want for Christmas (well, that and an iPod).

SCENE 1
1)   Who gives Beatrice heartburn?
2)   What combination of characters would make Beatrice's perfect man?
3)   What does Beatrice feel about men with beards?
4)   Antonio says to Hero, "Well, niece, I trust you will be ruled by your father." What is he hoping she'll do?
5)   Four couples join in with the dance — write down who they are.
6)   In lines 122-128 Beatrice heaps the insults on Benedick — write down three of them and explain what they mean.
7)   Who does Claudio pretend to be when he's talking to Don John?
8)   What dastardly lie does Don John tell Claudio?
9)   Does Claudio believe him?
10)   Why does Claudio flounce off when Benedick speaks to him?
11)   How does Benedick feel about Beatrice's description of him as "the Prince's jester"?
12)   Write out Benedick's rant about Beatrice (in lines 216-236) in your own words.
13)   In lines 238-246, what ridiculous things does Benedick offer to do, to avoid speaking to Beatrice?
14)   What does Beatrice mean when she says her heart stays "on the windy side of care"?
15)   When does Claudio want to get married? When does Leonato say would be a more sensible time?
16)   Who offers to help Don Pedro in his plan to get Beatrice married off? Write down three names.

SCENE 2
17)   Who offers to help Don John spoil the wedding?
18)   Why does Don John want to spoil it? Base your answer on lines 4-7.
19)   How much does Don John offer to pay for the help he is offered?

SCENE 3
20)   In lines 8-21 Benedick compares Claudio before he fell in love with Claudio after he fell in love. Write out two of the comparisons.
21)   Who is the "kid-fox" Claudio is talking about in line 40?
22)   What does Benedick think of Balthasar's song? Write down the exact words that tell you what he thinks.
23)   Does Benedick fall for the trick?
24)   In lines 210-211 Benedick says, "This can be no trick. The conference was sadly borne." Write this down in your own words.

It's Beatrice's turn to be hoodwinked. She overhears Hero and Ursula saying Benedick's in love with her and believes every word.

Proposing = *making plans*

discourse = *conversation*

steal = *sneak*

pleached bower = *shady shelter made of intertwined branches*

9-11 *"like a prince's favourites, who become proud, and then use their pride against the power that encouraged it in the first place"*

purpose = *plan*　　office = *job*

presently = *shortly*

15-17 *"Now, Ursula, when Beatrice comes, as we're walking up and down the alley we must talk only of Benedick."*

merit = *deserve*

hearsay = *rumour*

lapwing = *type of bird that flies in jerky movements close to the ground*

angling = *fishing*

29-31 *"That's how we're fishing for Beatrice, who has already hidden herself in the honeysuckle bower. Don't worry about my end of the conversation."*

32-33 *"Then let's go near her, so she won't miss a word of the trap we're setting for her."*

35-36 *"She acts like a wild hawk."*

new-trothed = *newly engaged*

40 *"They begged me to tell her about it"*

ACT 3 SCENE 1
Leonato's garden

Enter HERO, MARGARET *and* URSULA

HERO   Good Margaret, run thee to the parlour —
　　　There shalt thou find my cousin Beatrice
　　　Proposing with the Prince and Claudio.
　　　Whisper her ear and tell her, I and Ursula
　　　Walk in the orchard and our whole discourse　　　5
　　　Is all of her. Say that thou overheard'st us,
　　　And bid her steal into the pleached bower,
　　　Where honeysuckles, ripened by the sun,
　　　Forbid the sun to enter, like favourites,
　　　Made proud by princes, that advance their pride　　　10
　　　Against that power that bred it. There will she hide her,
　　　To listen our purpose. This is thy office —
　　　Bear thee well in it and leave us alone.

MARGARET   I'll make her come, I warrant you, presently.

Exit

HERO   Now, Ursula, when Beatrice doth come,　　　15
　　　As we do trace this alley up and down,
　　　Our talk must only be of Benedick.
　　　When I do name him, let it be thy part
　　　To praise him more than ever man did merit.
　　　My talk to thee must be how Benedick　　　20
　　　Is sick in love with Beatrice. Of this matter
　　　Is little Cupid's crafty arrow made,
　　　That only wounds by hearsay.

Enter BEATRICE, *behind*

　　　　　　　　　　　Now begin,
　　　For look where Beatrice, like a lapwing, runs
　　　Close by the ground, to hear our conference.　　　25

URSULA   The pleasant'st angling is to see the fish
　　　Cut with her golden oars the silver stream,
　　　And greedily devour the treacherous bait.
　　　So angle we for Beatrice, who even now
　　　Is couched in the woodbine coverture.　　　30
　　　Fear you not my part of the dialogue.

HERO   Then go we near her, that her ear lose nothing
　　　Of the false-sweet bait that we lay for it.

(approaching the bower)

　　　No, truly, Ursula, she is too disdainful.
　　　I know her spirits are as coy and wild　　　35
　　　As haggards of the rock.

URSULA　　　　　　　　But are you sure
　　　That Benedick loves Beatrice so entirely?

HERO   So says the Prince and my new-trothed lord.

URSULA   And did they bid you tell her of it, madam?

HERO   They did entreat me to acquaint her of it,　　　40
　　　But I persuaded them, if they loved Benedick,

To wish him wrestle with affection,
And never to let Beatrice know of it.

URSULA   Why did you so? Doth not the gentleman
   Deserve as full as fortunate a bed   45
   As ever Beatrice shall couch upon?

HERO   O god of love! I know he doth deserve
   As much as may be yielded to a man,
   But Nature never framed a woman's heart
   Of prouder stuff than that of Beatrice.   50
   Disdain and scorn ride sparkling in her eyes,
   Misprising what they look on, and her wit
   Values itself so highly that to her
   All matter else seems weak. She cannot love,
   Nor take no shape nor project of affection,   55
   She is so self-endeared.

URSULA   Sure, I think so,
   And therefore certainly it were not good
   She knew his love, lest she make sport at it.

HERO   Why, you speak truth. I never yet saw man,
   How wise, how noble, young, how rarely featured,   60
   But she would spell him backward. If fair-faced,
   She would swear the gentleman should be her sister;
   If black, why, Nature, drawing of an antic,
   Made a foul blot; if tall, a lance ill-headed;
   If low, an agate very vilely cut;   65
   If speaking, why, a vane blown with all winds;
   If silent, why, a block moved with none.
   So turns she every man the wrong side out
   And never gives to truth and virtue that
   Which simpleness and merit purchaseth.   70

URSULA   Sure, sure, such carping is not commendable.

HERO   No, not to be so odd and from all fashions
   As Beatrice is, cannot be commendable:
   But who dare tell her so? If I should speak,
   She would mock me into air. O, she would laugh me   75
   Out of myself, press me to death with wit.
   Therefore let Benedick, like covered fire,
   Consume away in sighs, waste inwardly.
   It were a better death than die with mocks,
   Which is as bad as die with tickling.   80

URSULA   Yet tell her of it, hear what she will say.

HERO   No. Rather I will go to Benedick
   And counsel him to fight against his passion.
   And, truly, I'll devise some honest slanders
   To stain my cousin with. One doth not know   85
   How much an ill word may empoison liking.

URSULA   O, do not do your cousin such a wrong.
   She cannot be so much without true judgment —
   Having so swift and excellent a wit
   As she is prized to have — as to refuse   90
   So rare a gentleman as Signior Benedick.

---

42   "suppress his feelings"

44-46   "Doesn't he deserve to be as lucky as the bed that has Beatrice lie on it?"

misprising = undervaluing

52-56   "she's so arrogant about her own brains that she thinks everyone else is stupid. She can't love, or give or receive affection, because she is so full of herself."

make sport at it = make fun of it

59-70   "I've never yet seen a man, no matter how wise, noble, young or handsome, who Beatrice hasn't found fault with. If he's fair-skinned, she'll swear the man should be her sister; if he's dark-skinned she'll say Nature was drawing a caricature and smudged the ink; if he's tall, he's an ugly-headed spear; if he's short, a badly cut gemstone; if he's talkative she'll say he's like a weather vane, blown by all the winds; and if he's quiet she'll say he's a block. She turns every man inside-out, and never gives credit where credit's due."

carping = criticism

odd, from all fashions = contrary

covered fire = covered fire (e.g. in a closed stove) does not burn brightly but burns very hot

counsel = advise

84-86   "I'll think up some lies to make him think worse of Beatrice. You never know how much a word of criticism can change someone's feelings."

92 "He's the best man in Italy" →

HERO   He is the only man of Italy,
Always excepted my dear Claudio.

*94-97 "Please don't be angry with →
me for giving my opinion —
Benedick, for looks, manners, brains
and bravery is said to be the best
man in Italy."*

URSULA   I pray you, be not angry with me, madam,
Speaking my fancy: Signior Benedick,   95
For shape, for bearing, argument and valour,
Goes foremost in report through Italy.

*98 "He's certainly got a →
very good reputation."*

HERO   Indeed, he hath an excellent good name.

URSULA   His excellence did earn it, ere he had it.
When are you married, madam?   100

*102-103 "I'll show you some
outfits and have your advice on →
which is best to wear tomorrow."*

HERO   Why, every day, to-morrow. Come, go in.
I'll show thee some attires, and have thy counsel
Which is the best to furnish me to-morrow.

*limed = caught (like a bird
in a sticky lime-glue trap)*

URSULA   She's limed, I warrant you: we have caught her,
madam.   105

*106 "If it turns out that way, →
then love is a chancy business"*

HERO   If it prove so, then loving goes by haps;
Some Cupid kills with arrows, some with traps.

Exeunt HERO *and* URSULA

*requite thee =
return your love*

BEATRICE *(coming forward)*
What fire is in mine ears? Can this be true?
Stand I condemned for pride and scorn so much?
Contempt, farewell, and maiden pride, adieu!   110
No glory lives behind the back of such.
And, Benedick, love on. I will requite thee,
Taming my wild heart to thy loving hand.

*114-117 "If you love me, I'll be nice to
you and we can get married — for →
others say you are worthy and I think
they're right."*

If thou dost love, my kindness shall incite thee
To bind our loves up in a holy band;   115
For others say thou dost deserve, and I
Believe it better than reportingly.

Exit

ACT 3   SCENE 2
A room in Leonato's house

Enter DON PEDRO, CLAUDIO, BENEDICK *and* LEONATO

DON PEDRO   I do but stay till your marriage be consummate, and then go I toward Aragon.

CLAUDIO   I'll bring you thither, my lord, if you'll vouchsafe me.

DON PEDRO   Nay, that would be as great a soil in the new gloss of your marriage as to show a child his new coat and forbid him to wear it. I will only be bold with Benedick for his company; for, from the crown of his head to the sole of his foot, he is all mirth. He hath twice or thrice cut Cupid's bow-string and the little hangman dare not shoot at him. He hath a heart as sound as a bell and his tongue is the clapper, for what his heart thinks his tongue speaks.

BENEDICK   Gallants, I am not as I have been.

LEONATO   So say I — methinks you are sadder.

CLAUDIO   I hope he be in love.

DON PEDRO   Hang him, truant! There's no true drop of blood in him, to be truly touched with love. If he be sad, he wants money.

BENEDICK   I have the toothache.

DON PEDRO   Draw it.

BENEDICK   Hang it!

CLAUDIO   You must hang it first, and draw it afterwards.

DON PEDRO   What! Sigh for the toothache?

LEONATO   Where is but a humour or a worm.

BENEDICK   Well, every one can master a grief but he that has it.

CLAUDIO   Yet say I, he is in love.

DON PEDRO   There is no appearance of fancy in him, unless it be a fancy that he hath to strange disguises; as, to be a Dutchman today, a Frenchman tomorrow, or in the shape of two countries at once, as, a German from the waist downward, all slops, and a Spaniard from the hip upward, no doublet. Unless he have a fancy to this foolery, as it appears he hath, he is no fool for fancy, as you would have it appear he is.

CLAUDIO   If he be not in love with some woman, there is no believing old signs. 'A brushes his hat o' mornings. What should that bode?

DON PEDRO   Hath any man seen him at the barber's?

5
10
15
20
25
30
35
40

consummate = *complete*

3-4 *"I'll go with you if you want."*

5-7 *"No, that would stain your shiny new marriage as much as it would upset a child to show him his new coat and forbid him to wear it."*

9-11 *"He's avoided love so much that Cupid's fed up of trying."*

clapper = *the dangly bit inside a bell that makes it sound*

gallants = *gentlemen*

truant = *tramp*

23 *This is a bit of a grisly word play. Claudio's making a pun on 'hung, drawn and quartered' — traitors were hung first, then had their guts dragged out, then were cut into four quarters. Nice.*

25 *People believed toothache was caused by mysterious gases (humours) or little worms that ate into the teeth.*

26-27 *"It's easy to rise above problems when they're not your own."*

29-30 *"He doesn't seem to be in love, unless it's a love for strange costumes."*

slops = *baggy trousers*

doublet = *jacket*

'a = *he*

bode = *lead to, foretell*

42-43 *"his old beard has been used to stuff tennis balls", i.e. he's gone to the barber for a shave. Claudio and Pedro think Benedick's trying to impress Beatrice by making himself look nice.*

46-47 *"No, he smothers himself with perfume. Can you sniff out what he's up to from that?"*

51 *"When has he ever washed his face?"*

52-53 *"Yes, or to wear make-up? That's what people are saying about him."*

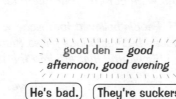

54-55 *"No, the clearest proof is his sense of humour, he's singing love songs instead of using his wit." 'Stops' on a lute are like frets on a guitar.*

ill conditions = bad habits

charm = cure

break with him = break the news to him

good den = good afternoon, good evening

He's bad. They're suckers.

82 *"I'm not sure he will want to marry tomorrow when he knows what I know."*

83-84 *"If there's a problem, then tell me what it is."*

CLAUDIO No, but the barber's man hath been seen with him, and the old ornament of his cheek hath already stuffed tennis balls.

LEONATO Indeed, he looks younger than he did, by the loss of a beard. 45

DON PEDRO Nay, a' rubs himself with civet. Can you smell him out by that?

CLAUDIO That's as much as to say, the sweet youth's in love.

DON PEDRO The greatest note of it is his melancholy. 50

CLAUDIO And when was he wont to wash his face?

DON PEDRO Yea, or to paint himself? For the which, I hear what they say of him.

CLAUDIO Nay, but his jesting spirit, which is now crept into a lute-string, and now governed by stops. 55

DON PEDRO Indeed, that tells a heavy tale for him. Conclude, conclude he is in love.

CLAUDIO Nay, but I know who loves him.

DON PEDRO That would I know too. I warrant, one that knows him not. 60

CLAUDIO Yes, and his ill conditions, and, in despite of all, dies for him.

DON PEDRO She shall be buried with her face upwards.

BENEDICK Yet is this no charm for the toothache. Old signior, walk aside with me. I have studied eight or nine 65 wise words to speak to you, which these hobby-horses must not hear.

Exeunt BENEDICK *and* LEONATO

DON PEDRO For my life, to break with him about Beatrice.

CLAUDIO 'Tis even so. Hero and Margaret have by this played their parts with Beatrice, and then the two bears 70 will not bite one another when they meet.

Enter DON JOHN

DON JOHN My lord and brother, God save you!

DON PEDRO Good den, brother.

DON JOHN If your leisure served, I would speak with you.

DON PEDRO In private? 75

DON JOHN If it please you, yet Count Claudio may hear, for what I would speak of concerns him.

DON PEDRO What's the matter?

DON JOHN *(to Claudio)* Means your lordship to be married tomorrow? 80

DON PEDRO You know he does.

DON JOHN I know not that, when he knows what I know.

CLAUDIO If there be any impediment, I pray you discover it.

DON JOHN You may think I love you not. Let that appear 85 hereafter, and aim better at me by that I now will

---

manifest. For my brother, I think he holds you well, and in dearness of heart hath holp to effect your ensuing marriage — surely suit ill-spent and labour ill-bestowed.

85-89 "You may think I don't like you. You'll hold a better opinion of me when you've heard what I've got to say. My brother thinks highly of you, and has helped arrange your marriage — surely a misguided effort and a waste of time."

DON PEDRO   Why, what's the matter?   90

DON JOHN   I came hither to tell you, and, circumstances shortened, for she has been too long a talking of, the lady is disloyal.

91-93 "To cut a long story short, Hero's having an affair."

CLAUDIO   Who, Hero?

DON PEDRO   Even she — Leonato's Hero, your Hero, every man's Hero.   95

CLAUDIO   Disloyal?

DON JOHN   The word is too good to paint out her wickedness. I could say she were worse; think you of a worse title, and I will fit her to it. Wonder not till further warrant. Go but with me tonight, you shall see her chamber window entered, even the night before her wedding day. If you love her then, tomorrow wed her; but it would better fit your honour to change your mind.   100

98-104 "'Disloyal' is too good a word to describe her wickedness. Don't think any more about it till you've got proof. Go with me tonight and you will see a man go in by her bedroom window, the very night before her wedding day. If you still love her then, marry her tomorrow, but it would be a better idea to change your mind."

CLAUDIO   May this be so?   105

DON PEDRO   I will not think it.

DON JOHN   If you dare not trust that you see, confess not that you know. If you will follow me, I will show you enough, and when you have seen more and heard more, proceed accordingly.   110

107-110 "If you won't believe what you see you can't claim to know. If you come with me I'll give you proof and you can decide what to do."

CLAUDIO   If I see any thing tonight why I should not marry her, tomorrow in the congregation, where I should wed, there will I shame her.

thing = *reason*

DON PEDRO   And, as I wooed for thee to obtain her, I will join with thee to disgrace her.   115

DON JOHN   I will disparage her no farther till you are my witnesses. Bear it coldly but till midnight, and let the issue show itself.

116-118 "I won't say any more against her till you've seen the proof. Keep it to yourselves till midnight, and then let the story come out."

DON PEDRO   O day untowardly turned!

CLAUDIO   O mischief strangely thwarting!   120

DON JOHN   O plague right well prevented! So will you say when you have seen the sequel.

Exeunt

sequel = *what's to follow*

Dogberry and Verges brief the Watch on their night time guard duties. The Watch overhear Borachio boasting to Conrade about the dastardly plan to spoil Hero and Claudio's wedding.

ACT 3   SCENE 3
A street

Enter DOGBERRY and VERGES with the Watch

DOGBERRY Are you good men and true?

VERGES Yea, or else it were pity but they should suffer salvation, body and soul.

DOGBERRY Nay, that were a punishment too good for them, if they should have any allegiance in them, being chosen for the Prince's Watch.   5

VERGES Well, give them their charge, neighbour Dogberry.

DOGBERRY First, who think you the most desertless man to be constable?   10

FIRST WATCHMAN Hugh Otecake, sir, or George Seacole, for they can write and read.

DOGBERRY Come hither, neighbour Seacole. God hath blessed you with a good name — to be a well-favoured man is the gift of fortune, but to write and read comes   15
by nature.

SECOND WATCHMAN Both which, master constable —

DOGBERRY You have — I knew it would be your answer. Well, for your favour, sir, why, give God thanks, and make no boast of it; and for your writing and reading,   20
let that appear when there is no need of such vanity. You are thought here to be the most senseless and fit man for the constable of the Watch — therefore bear you the lantern. This is your charge: you shall comprehend all vagrom men; you are to bid any man   25
stand, in the Prince's name.

SECOND WATCHMAN How if a' will not stand?

DOGBERRY Why, then, take no note of him, but let him go, and presently call the rest of the Watch together and thank God you are rid of a knave.   30

VERGES If he will not stand when he is bidden, he is none of the Prince's subjects.

DOGBERRY True, and they are to meddle with none but the Prince's subjects. You shall also make no noise in the streets, for, for the Watch to babble and to talk is   35
most tolerable and not to be endured.

WATCHMAN We will rather sleep than talk: we know what belongs to a Watch.

DOGBERRY Why, you speak like an ancient and most quiet watchman, for I cannot see how sleeping should   40
offend. Only, have a care that your bills be not stolen. Well, you are to call at all the ale-houses, and bid those that are drunk get them to bed.

---

3 The Watch are a bunch of bumbling policeman. When they use big words they tend to get them wrong — here he means damnation not salvation.

Blah, blah, blah, blah, blah, blah...

charge = orders

desertless = undeserving

14 Sea coal was good quality coal, imported by ship.

well-favoured = good looking

24-26 "Here are your orders: you shall arrest all vagrants and you shall order any man you see to stop."

27 "What if he won't stop?"

28-30 "Then ignore him, and let him go, then call the rest of the Watch together and thank God that you have got rid of a rascal."

31 "If he won't stop when you ask him."

33-34 "they mustn't interfere with anyone except the Prince's subjects"

bills = long poles with hooks on the ends — the watchmen's weapons

ale-houses = pubs

WATCHMAN   How if they will not?

DOGBERRY   Why, then, let them alone till they are sober. 45
If they make you not then the better answer, you may
say they are not the men you took them for.

WATCHMAN   Well, sir.

DOGBERRY   If you meet a thief, you may suspect him, by
virtue of your office, to be no true man, and, for such 50
kind of men, the less you meddle or make with them,
why the more is for your honesty.

51-52 "the less you have to do with people like that, the more honest you will appear"

WATCHMAN   If we know him to be a thief, shall we not lay
hands on him?

DOGBERRY   Truly, by your office, you may, but I think they 55
that touch pitch will be defiled. The most peaceable
way for you, if you do take a thief, is to let him show
himself what he is and steal out of your company.

55-56 "You're entitled to arrest him, but you can't touch tar without getting dirty."

VERGES   You have been always called a merciful man,
partner. 60

DOGBERRY   Truly, I would not hang a dog by my will,
much more a man who hath any honesty in him.

VERGES   If you hear a child cry in the night, you must call
to the nurse and bid her still it.

still it = quieten it down

WATCHMAN   How if the nurse be asleep and will not hear 65
us?

65-66 "What if the nurse is asleep and can't hear us?"

DOGBERRY   Why, then, depart in peace, and let the child
wake her with crying, for the ewe that will not hear her
lamb when it baas will never answer a calf when he
bleats. 70

VERGES   'Tis very true.

DOGBERRY   This is the end of the charge. You,
constable, are to present the Prince's own person. If
you meet the Prince in the night, you may stay him.

72-74 "You, constable, deal with the Prince himself. If you meet the Prince in the night you have the right to detain him."

VERGES   Nay, by'r our lady, that I think a' cannot. 75

DOGBERRY   Five shillings to one on't, with any man that
knows the statutes, he may stay him! Marry, not without
the Prince be willing, for, indeed, the Watch ought to
offend no man, and it is an offence to stay a man
against his will. 80

statutes = laws

VERGES   By'r lady, I think it be so.

DOGBERRY   Ha, ah, ha! Well, masters, good night. An
there be any matter of weight chances, call up me.
Keep your fellows' counsels and your own, and good
night. Come, neighbour. 85

82-84 "If anything important happens, come and get me. Follow your companions' good advice and your own."

WATCHMAN   Well, masters, we hear our charge. Let us
go sit here upon the church-bench till two, and then all
to bed.

DOGBERRY   One word more, honest neighbours. I pray
you watch about Signior Leonato's door, for the wedding 90
being there tomorrow, there is a great coil to-night.
Adieu: be vigitant, I beseech you.

coil = stir, to-do

Exeunt DOGBERRY *and* VERGES

93 "Oi, Conrade!" Borachio can't see Conrade in the dark.

94 "Shhh! Don't move a muscle." The Watchman's talking to the other members of the watch.

97-98 "I say, I had such an itchy elbow — I thought there would be a scab." A scab can also mean a low-life criminal. Itches were supposed to be a sign that some bad person was about to turn up.

penthouse = *overhanging roof*

104-105 "Don't do anything yet."

108 "Is it possible that any crime should be that expensive?"

109-112 "You should be asking if it's possible that any crime should be that valuable — for when rich villains need the help of poor ones, the poor ones can charge what they like."

114 "That shows you are inexperienced."

hot bloods = *fashionable young men*

Pharaoh's soldiers = *soldiers who chased the Jews when they were escaping from Egypt in the Bible*

reechy = *grimy*

Bel's priests = *priests killed by the Jewish king Daniel for worshipping a false God (another Bible story)*

smirched = *dirty*

massy = *big*

Enter BORACHIO *and* CONRADE

BORACHIO What, Conrade!

WATCHMAN *(aside)* Peace! Stir not.

BORACHIO Conrade, I say!   95

CONRADE Here, man. I am at thy elbow.

BORACHIO Mass, and my elbow itched — I thought there would a scab follow.

CONRADE I will owe thee an answer for that; and now forward with thy tale.   100

BORACHIO Stand thee close, then, under this penthouse, for it drizzles rain, and I will, like a true drunkard, utter all to thee.

WATCHMAN *(aside)* Some treason, masters — yet stand close.   105

BORACHIO Therefore know I have earned of Don John a thousand ducats.

CONRADE Is it possible that any villainy should be so dear?

BORACHIO Thou shouldst rather ask if it were possible any villainy should be so rich; for when rich villains have need of poor ones, poor ones may make what price they will.   110

CONRADE I wonder at it.

BORACHIO That shows thou art unconfirmed. Thou knowest that the fashion of a doublet, or a hat, or a cloak, is nothing to a man.   115

CONRADE Yes, it is apparel.

BORACHIO I mean, the fashion.

CONRADE Yes, the fashion is the fashion.

BORACHIO Tush! I may as well say the fool's the fool. But seest thou not what a deformed thief this fashion is?   120

WATCHMAN *(aside)* I know that Deformed. A' has been a vile thief this seven year — a' goes up and down like a gentleman. I remember his name.

BORACHIO Didst thou not hear somebody?   125

CONRADE No. 'Twas the vane on the house.

BORACHIO Seest thou not, I say, what a deformed thief this fashion is? How giddily a' turns about all the hot bloods between fourteen and five-and-thirty, sometimes fashioning them like Pharaoh's soldiers in the reechy painting, sometime like god Bel's priests in the old church-window, sometime like the shaven Hercules in the smirched worm-eaten tapestry, where his codpiece seems as massy as his club?   130

CONRADE All this I see, and I see that the fashion wears out more apparel than the man. But art not thou thyself giddy with the fashion too, that thou hast shifted out of thy tale into telling me of the fashion?   135

BORACHIO Not so, neither. But know that I have tonight wooed Margaret, the lady Hero's gentlewoman, by the   140

name of Hero. She leans me out at her mistress'
chamber-window, bids me a thousand times goodnight
— I tell this tale vilely — I should first tell thee how the
Prince, Claudio and my master, planted and placed and
possessed by my master Don John, saw afar off in the   145
orchard this amiable encounter.

CONRADE And thought they Margaret was Hero?

BORACHIO Two of them did, the Prince and Claudio; but
the devil my master knew she was Margaret; and partly
by his oaths, which first possessed them, partly by the   150
dark night, which did deceive them, but chiefly by my
villainy, which did confirm any slander that Don John
had made, away went Claudio enraged, swore he would
meet her, as he was appointed, next morning at the
temple, and there, before the whole congregation,   155
shame her with what he saw o'ernight and send her
home again without a husband.

FIRST WATCHMAN We charge you, in the Prince's name,
stand!

SECOND WATCHMAN Call up the right master constable.   160
We have here recovered the most dangerous piece of
lechery that ever was known in the commonwealth.

FIRST WATCHMAN And one Deformed is one of them. I
know him — a' wears a lock.

CONRADE Masters, masters —   165

SECOND WATCHMAN You'll be made bring Deformed
forth, I warrant you.

CONRADE Masters —

FIRST WATCHMAN Never speak, we charge you. Let us
obey you to go with us.   170

BORACHIO We are like to prove a goodly commodity,
being taken up of these men's bills.

CONRADE A commodity in question, I warrant you.
Come, we'll obey you.

Exeunt

143 "I'm not telling this story very well"

amiable encounter = friendly meeting

the devil my master =
he means Don John

possessed = took hold of

temple = church

161-162 "We've found the worst crime ever seen in this republic."

164 A lock of hair, grown extra-long, so men could tie bits of ribbon in, given them by their girlfriends. Not the greatest of English hair fashions.

171-172 A pun — "We'll end up like goods displayed for sale, when we're taken up on these men's billhooks," or "We'll end up like goods bought on credit, when we've been charged with these men's bills." Bills can mean money or the watchmen's weapons.

commodity = something valuable

Act 3, Scene 3

38

Hero and the other girls are getting ready for the wedding. Beatrice is feeling a bit peculiar on account of being in love with Benedick, but everyone else is in a very jolly mood.

ACT 3   SCENE 4
Hero's apartment

Enter HERO, MARGARET and URSULA

1-2 *"Ask her to get out of bed."*

HERO   Good Ursula, wake my cousin Beatrice, and desire her to rise.

URSULA   I will, lady.

HERO   And bid her come hither.

hither = here

URSULA   Well.   5

Exit

troth = to be honest

rebato = ruff

MARGARET   Troth, I think your other rebato were better.

HERO   No, pray thee, good Meg, I'll wear this.

MARGARET   By my troth, 's not so good, and I warrant your cousin will say so.

HERO   My cousin's a fool, and thou art another: I'll wear none but this.   10

tire = headdress

hair = hair extensions attached to the ruff

MARGARET   I like the new tire within excellently, if the hair were a thought browner; and your gown's a most rare fashion, i' faith. I saw the Duchess of Milan's gown that they praise so.   15

16 *"They say that was more impressive."*

HERO   O, that exceeds, they say.

17-21 *"Goodness, it's just a dressing gown compared to yours: cloth of gold, slashes, embroidered with silver and pearls, down sleeves, side sleeves, and skirts trimmed with bluish tinsel; but yours is much better."*

MARGARET   By my troth, 's but a night-gown in respect of yours: cloth o' gold, and cuts, and laced with silver, set with pearls, down sleeves, side sleeves and skirts, round underborne with a bluish tinsel; but for a fine, quaint, graceful and excellent fashion, yours is worth ten on 't.   20

22-23 *A heavy heart was supposed to be a sign that something bad was about to happen.*

HERO   God give me joy to wear it, for my heart is exceeding heavy!

MARGARET   'Twill be heavier soon by the weight of a man.

HERO   Fie upon thee! Art not ashamed?   25

28-30 *"I think you would rather I said, to sound more respectful, 'a husband'. If bad thoughts do not twist the meaning of true words, I'll offend nobody."*

MARGARET   Of what, lady? Of speaking honourably? Is not marriage honourable in a beggar? Is not your lord honourable without marriage? I think you would have me say, saving your reverence, 'a husband'. And bad thinking do not wrest true speaking, I'll offend nobody. Is there any harm in 'the heavier for a husband'? None, I think, and it be the right husband and the right wife, otherwise 'tis light, and not heavy. Ask my Lady Beatrice else — here she comes.   30

Enter BEATRICE

37 *"Are you feeling out of sorts?"*

HERO   Good morrow, coz.   35

BEATRICE   Good morrow, sweet Hero.

HERO   Why how now? Do you speak in the sick tune?

39-40 *"Let's sing 'Light of love' — that doesn't have a burden." A 'burden' was a deep bass part for male voices.*

BEATRICE   I am out of all other tune, methinks.

41 *"You're the ones who are light of love"*

MARGARET   Clap's into 'Light o' love' — that goes without a burden. Do you sing it, and I'll dance it.   40

heels = a 'light-heeled' woman would sleep with anyone

41-43 *"If your husband has enough stables, you'll see he'll have enough barns too." 'Barns' can also mean 'children', like the Scottish word 'bairns'.*

BEATRICE   Ye light o' love, with your heels! Then, if your husband have stables enough, you'll see he shall lack no barns.

Act 3, Scene 4

MARGARET O illegitimate construction! I scorn that with my heels. 45

44-45 "That's really twisting the words! I'm walking away."

BEATRICE 'Tis almost five o'clock, cousin. 'Tis time you were ready. By my troth, I am exceeding ill. Heigh-ho!

MARGARET For a hawk, a horse, or a husband?

BEATRICE For the letter that begins them all, H.

MARGARET Well, and you be not turned Turk, there's no more sailing by the star. 50

50-51 "Well, I'm as sure you've changed as sailors are sure of the North star."

BEATRICE What means the fool, trow?

trow = do you think

MARGARET Nothing I — but God send every one their heart's desire!

HERO These gloves the count sent me — they are an excellent perfume. 55

57 "I've got a blocked nose, cousin. I can't smell it."

BEATRICE I am stuffed, cousin. I cannot smell.

MARGARET A maid, and stuffed! There's goodly catching of cold.

58-59 "A virgin who's had a good stuffing!" Stuffing can mean pregnant.

BEATRICE O, God help me! God help me! How long have you professed apprehension? 60

60-61 "When did you start claiming to be quick on the uptake?"

MARGARET Ever since you left it. Doth not my wit become me rarely?

62-63 "Ever since you stopped being witty. Doesn't my wit suit me?"

BEATRICE It is not seen enough, you should wear it in your cap. By my troth, I am sick. 65

MARGARET Get you some of this distilled Carduus Benedictus, and lay it to your heart — it is the only thing for a qualm.

66-68 "Try some of this distilled Carduus Benedictus (medicine made from holy thistle) and lay it by your heart — it's the only cure for a funny turn."

HERO There thou prickest her with a thistle.

BEATRICE Benedictus! Why Benedictus? You have some moral in this Benedictus. 70

70-71 "What point are you trying to make with this Benedictus?"

MARGARET Moral! No, by my troth, I have no moral meaning; I meant, plain holy thistle. You may think perchance that I think you are in love. Nay, by'r lady, I am not such a fool to think what I list, nor I list not to 75 think what I can, nor indeed I cannot think, if I would think my heart out of thinking, that you are in love or that you will be in love or that you can be in love. Yet Benedick was such another, and now is he become a man: he swore he would never marry, and yet now, in 80 despite of his heart, he eats his meat without grudging: and how you may be converted I know not, but methinks you look with your eyes as other women do.

73-78 "Maybe you think I think you're in love. No, I'm not such a fool as to let myself believe what I want to believe, nor do I want to believe what I can believe, nor can I believe, even if I prevent my heart from thinking, that you are in love or will be in love or can be in love."

81 "Has a good appetite."

BEATRICE What pace is this that thy tongue keeps?

84 "Why are you rattling on like this?"

MARGARET Not a false gallop. 85

Re-enter URSULA

URSULA Madam, withdraw — the prince, the count, Signior Benedick, Don John, and all the gallants of the town, are come to fetch you to church.

withdraw = leave the room

gallants = gentlemen

HERO Help to dress me, good coz, good Meg, good Ursula. 90

Exeunt

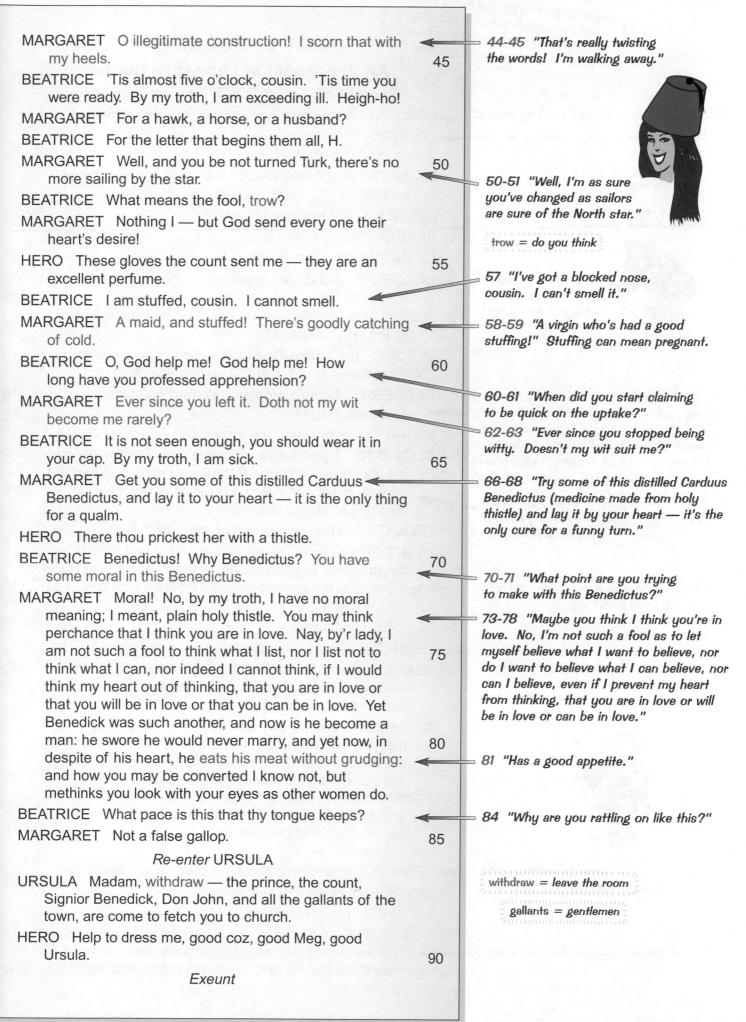

Act 3, Scene 4

Dogberry and Verges try to tell Leonato about Don John's evil plot, but they're really slow getting to the point and Leonato goes off to the wedding.

ACT 3   SCENE 5
Another room in Leonato's house
Enter LEONATO, *with* DOGBERRY *and* VERGES

1 "What do you want with me, neighbour?"

LEONATO   What would you with me, honest neighbour?

2-3 "I'd like a word in private, sir, on a matter that affects you personally." He is using the wrong words again — he uses decerns when he means concerns.

DOGBERRY   Marry, sir, I would have some confidence with you that decerns you nearly.

You're only as old as Dogberry makes you feel.

LEONATO   Brief, I pray you, for you see it is a busy time with me.   5

DOGBERRY   Marry, this it is, sir.

VERGES   Yes, in truth it is, sir.

LEONATO   What is it, my good friends?

9-10 "Mr. Verges tends to wander off the point a bit, sir"

DOGBERRY   Goodman Verges, sir, speaks a little off the matter: an old man, sir, and his wits are not so blunt as,   10
God help, I would desire they were, but, in faith, honest as the skin between his brows.

VERGES   Yes, I thank God I am as honest as any man living that is an old man and no honester than I.

15-16 Dogberry says odorous (meaning 'smelly') when he means 'odious' ('hateful'). Palabras is Dogberry's version of the Spanish phrase 'pocas palabras' meaning 'a few words' — a bit like the English phrase 'least said, soonest mended'.

DOGBERRY   Comparisons are odorous: palabras,   15
neighbour Verges.

LEONATO   Neighbours, you are tedious.

DOGBERRY   It pleases your worship to say so, but we are the poor duke's officers. But truly, for mine own part, if I were as tedious as a king, I could find in my heart to   20
bestow it all of your worship.

19-21 "For my part, if I was as tedious as a king, I would find it in my heart to give all my tediousness to you."

an = if

LEONATO   All thy tediousness on me, ah?

DOGBERRY   Yea, an 'twere a thousand pound more than 'tis; for I hear as good exclamation on your worship as of
any man in the city and though I be but a poor man, I am   25
glad to hear it.

24-25 "I hear as good things said about you as about any man in the city"

VERGES   And so am I.

28 "I'd love to know what it is you're going to tell me."

LEONATO   I would fain know what you have to say.

VERGES   Marry, sir, our Watch tonight, excepting your worship's presence, ha' ta'en a couple of as arrant   30
knaves as any in Messina.

arrant knaves = complete villians

Blah, blah, blah, blah, blah, blah...

DOGBERRY   A good old man, sir. He will be talking — as they say 'when the age is in, the wit is out'. God help us, it is a world to see! Well said, i' faith, neighbour Verges. Well, God's a good man; an two men ride of a horse,   35
one must ride behind. An honest soul, i' faith, sir; by my troth he is, as ever broke bread; but God is to be worshipped — all men are not alike, alas, good neighbour!

40 "Certainly, neighbour, he doesn't match your standards."

LEONATO   Indeed, neighbour, he comes too short of you.   40

DOGBERRY   Gifts that God gives.

LEONATO   I must leave you.

DOGBERRY   One word, sir: our Watch, sir, have indeed comprehended two aspicious persons, and we would have them this morning examined before your worship.   45

44 Dogberry-speak for 'suspicious'.

LEONATO Take their examination yourself and bring it me:
   I am now in great haste, as it may appear unto you.

DOGBERRY It shall be suffigance.

LEONATO Drink some wine ere you go. Fare you well!

Enter a Messenger

MESSENGER My lord, they stay for you to give your   50
   daughter to her husband.

LEONATO I'll wait upon them: I am ready.

Exeunt LEONATO and Messenger

DOGBERRY Go, good partner, go, get you to Francis
   Seacole — bid him bring his pen and inkhorn to the
   gaol: we are now to examination these men.   55

VERGES And we must do it wisely.

DOGBERRY We will spare for no wit, I warrant you.
   Here's that shall drive some of them to a non-come:
   only get the learned writer to set down our
   excommunication and meet me at the gaol.   60

Exeunt

46-47 "Take their statement yourself and bring it to me — I'm in a massive hurry, as you can probably tell."

48 A nonsense word.

50-51 "They're waiting for you to give away your daughter,"

gaol = jail

58 "We'll drive some of them into a state of confusion"

60 He means 'communication'.

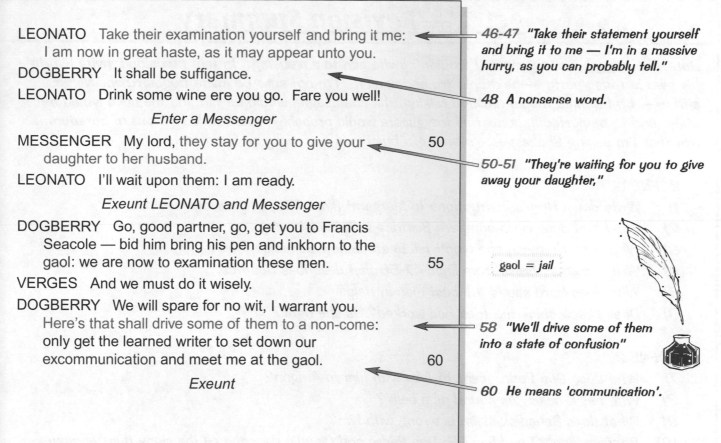

Act 3, Scene 5

Act 3 — Revision Summary

Don John is _such_ a nasty man. I wouldn't invite him to a wedding. In fact I wouldn't invite him to his own birthday party — he'd only try and spoil it. I'm not sure I'd invite Dogberry and Verges either — by the time they'd finished talking, the champagne would be flat and the cake would be stale, and to be perfectly honest all the guests would probably have nodded off out of boredom... Not that I'm saying Shakespeare's boring... but those two really do bang on...

SCENE 1

1) Write down Hero's instructions to Margaret (lines 1-13) in your own words.
2) What bird does Hero compare Beatrice to? Explain why.
3) Why does Hero say she won't tell Beatrice how Benedick feels?
4) Write down a phrase from lines 47-56 that describes Beatrice.
5) Who does Hero say is the best man in Italy?
6) Does Ursula think the trick has worked? Is she right?

SCENE 2

7) Who does Don Pedro want to take with him to Aragon?
8) Who has a heart "as sound as a bell"?
9) What does Benedick claim is wrong with him?
10) Between line 37 and line 55, Don Pedro and Claudio describe all the signs they've seen that Benedick's in love. Write down four of them.
11) How does Don John offer to prove that Hero is being unfaithful to Claudio?
12) Does Claudio believe him?

SCENE 3

13) Why are Hugh Otecake and George Seacole nominated as constables for the Watch?
14) What does Dogberry advise the Watch to do if they order someone to stop and he won't?
15) What does he advise them to do if they hear a baby crying?
16) Where does Dogberry order the Watch to take particular care tonight?
17) When Conrade and Borachio come in, do they realise the Watch are there?
18) Who saw Borachio talking to Margaret at Hero's window? Name three people.

SCENE 4

19) Where's Beatrice at the beginning of the scene?
20) What are Margaret and Hero doing?
21) When Beatrice comes in she isn't feeling her usual cheery self. What reason does she eventually give for this?
22) Who annoys Beatrice by prattling on?

SCENE 5

23) Write down a word from this scene that Dogberry gets wrong.
24) Who is quicker to get to the point — Dogberry or Verges?
25) Does Leonato wait to hear the full story?
26) Who do Dogberry and Verges plan to 'examination'?

ACT 4 SCENE 1
A church

Enter DON PEDRO, DON JOHN, LEONATO, FRIAR FRANCIS, CLAUDIO, BENEDICK, HERO, BEATRICE
and Attendants

LEONATO Come, Friar Francis, be brief. Only to the plain form of marriage, and you shall recount their particular duties afterwards.

FRIAR FRANCIS You come hither, my lord, to marry this lady? 　　5

CLAUDIO No.

LEONATO To be married to her. Friar, you come to marry her.

FRIAR FRANCIS Lady, you come hither to be married to this count? 　　10

HERO I do.

FRIAR FRANCIS If either of you know any inward impediment why you should not be conjoined, I charge you, on your souls, to utter it.

CLAUDIO Know you any, Hero? 　　15

HERO None, my lord.

FRIAR FRANCIS Know you any, count?

LEONATO I dare make his answer — none.

CLAUDIO O, what men dare do! What men may do!
　　What men daily do, not knowing what they do! 　　20

BENEDICK How now! Interjections? Why, then, some be of laughing, as, ah, ha, he!

CLAUDIO Stand thee by, friar. Father, by your leave,
　　Will you with free and unconstrained soul
　　Give me this maid, your daughter? 　　25

LEONATO As freely, son, as God did give her me.

CLAUDIO And what have I to give you back, whose worth
　　May counterpoise this rich and precious gift?

DON PEDRO Nothing, unless you render her again.

CLAUDIO Sweet Prince, you learn me noble thankfulness. 　　30
　　There, Leonato, take her back again:
　　Give not this rotten orange to your friend —
　　She's but the sign and semblance of her honour.
　　Behold how like a maid she blushes here!
　　O, what authority and show of truth 　　35
　　Can cunning sin cover itself withal!
　　Comes not that blood as modest evidence
　　To witness simple virtue? Would you not swear,
　　All you that see her, that she were a maid,
　　By these exterior shows? But she is none: 　　40
　　She knows the heat of a luxurious bed,
　　Her blush is guiltiness, not modesty.

LEONATO What do you mean, my lord?

1-3 *"Let's keep it snappy, Friar Francis. Just do the simple version of the service, and give them the lecture on how they should behave afterwards."*

GRRR...

12-14 *"If either of you know of any reason why you should not be married, I order you to reveal it now."*

18 *"I can answer for him — none."*

21-22 *Benedick tries to make a joke of Claudio's interruption.*

23-25 *"Hold on, friar. Are you giving me this girl, your daughter, with a clear and untroubled conscience?"*

counterpoise = *balance*

render her again = *give her back again*

30 *"You have taught me to be truly grateful."*

33-42 *"She only has the appearance of honour. Look, she's blushing like a virgin! Cunning sin disguises itself so convincingly! Isn't blushing supposed to be proof of chaste innocence? Wouldn't all you who see her here swear that she's a virgin, judging by her appearance? She certainly isn't though — she's felt the heat of a sinful bed, her blush is a sign of guilt not chastity."*

46-48 "Dear Claudio, if you yourself have taken her virginity —"

49-55 "I know what you're going to say. If I have slept with her, you'll say she only did it because I was going to be her husband, so it's not really a sin. No, Leonato. I never tempted her to go too far, but treated her with sweetness and gentle love, like a brother with his sister."

57-61 "Get lost, fake! Here's my argument. You act all sweet and innocent, but you're really a right tart."

63 "Are you ill, speaking like that?"

64-66 "What should I say? I've been dishonoured by trying to put my friend together with a common slut."

74-76 "Let me put just one question to your daughter. Use your influence with her to get her to answer truthfully."

77 "I order you, as my child, to give a true answer."

78-79 "Everyone's turned on me! Why are you interrogating me like this?"

81-82 "Who can harm my reputation with any truthful accusation?"

CLAUDIO Not to be married, not to knit my soul
To an approved wanton.   45

LEONATO Dear my lord, if you, in your own proof,
Have vanquished the resistance of her youth,
And made defeat of her virginity —

CLAUDIO I know what you would say. If I have known her,
You will say she did embrace me as a husband,   50
And so extenuate the forehand sin.
No, Leonato.
I never tempted her with word too large,
But, as a brother to his sister, showed
Bashful sincerity and comely love.   55

HERO And seemed I ever otherwise to you?

CLAUDIO Out on thee, seeming! I will write against it.
You seem to me as Dian in her orb,
As chaste as is the bud ere it be blown;
But you are more intemperate in your blood   60
Than Venus, or those pampered animals
That rage in savage sensuality.

HERO Is my lord well, that he doth speak so wide?

LEONATO Sweet Prince, why speak not you?

DON PEDRO   What should I speak?
I stand dishonoured, that have gone about   65
To link my dear friend to a common stale.

LEONATO Are these things spoken, or do I but dream?

DON JOHN Sir, they are spoken, and these things are true.

BENEDICK This looks not like a nuptial.

HERO   True! O God!

CLAUDIO Leonato, stand I here?   70
Is this the Prince? Is this the Prince's brother?
Is this face Hero's? Are our eyes our own?

LEONATO All this is so: but what of this, my lord?

CLAUDIO Let me but move one question to your daughter,
And, by that fatherly and kindly power   75
That you have in her, bid her answer truly.

LEONATO I charge thee do so, as thou art my child.

HERO O, God defend me! How am I beset!
What kind of catechising call you this?

CLAUDIO To make you answer truly to your name.   80

HERO Is it not Hero? Who can blot that name
With any just reproach?

CLAUDIO   Marry, that can Hero;
Hero itself can blot out Hero's virtue.
What man was he talked with you yesternight
Out at your window betwixt twelve and one?   85
Now, if you are a maid, answer to this.

HERO I talked with no man at that hour, my lord.

DON PEDRO Why, then are you no maiden. Leonato,
I am sorry you must hear — upon mine honour,

Myself, my brother and this grieved count   90
Did see her, hear her, at that hour last night
Talk with a ruffian at her chamber-window,
Who hath indeed, most like a liberal villain,
Confessed the vile encounters they have had
A thousand times in secret.   95

DON JOHN   Fie, fie, they are not to be named, my lord,
Not to be spoke of!
There is not chastity enough in language
Without offence to utter them. Thus, pretty lady,
I am sorry for thy much misgovernment.   100

CLAUDIO   O Hero, what a Hero hadst thou been,
If half thy outward graces had been placed
About thy thoughts and counsels of thy heart!
But fare thee well, most foul, most fair! Farewell,
Thou pure impiety and impious purity!   105
For thee I'll lock up all the gates of love,
And on my eyelids shall conjecture hang,
To turn all beauty into thoughts of harm,
And never shall it more be gracious.

LEONATO   Hath no man's dagger here a point for me?   110

HERO *swoons*

BEATRICE   Why, how now, cousin! Wherefore sink you
down?

DON JOHN   Come, let us go. These things, come thus to
Light, smother her spirits up.

Exeunt DON PEDRO, DON JOHN *and* CLAUDIO

BENEDICK   How doth the lady?

BEATRICE   Dead, I think. Help, uncle!   115
Hero! Why, Hero! Uncle! Signior Benedick! Friar!

LEONATO   O Fate! Take not away thy heavy hand.
Death is the fairest cover for her shame
That may be wished for.

BEATRICE   How now, cousin Hero!

FRIAR FRANCIS   Have comfort, lady.   120

LEONATO   Dost thou look up?

FRIAR FRANCIS   Yea, wherefore should she not?

LEONATO   Wherefore! Why, doth not every earthly thing
Cry shame upon her? Could she here deny
The story that is printed in her blood?
Do not live, Hero, do not ope thine eyes,   125
For, did I think thou wouldst not quickly die,
Thought I thy spirits were stronger than thy shames,
Myself would, on the rearward of reproaches,
Strike at thy life. Grieved I, I had but one?
Chid I for that at frugal nature's frame?   130
O, one too much by thee! Why had I one?
Why ever wast thou lovely in my eyes?
Why had I not with charitable hand
Took up a beggar's issue at my gates,

93-95 *"who has, like a shameless rascal, confessed to their many secret meetings"*

98-100 *"There isn't pure enough language to describe it without causing offence. I'm sorry, pretty lady, that you have behaved so badly."*

101-103 *"Oh Hero, what a Hero you would have been, if your behaviour was half as good as your appearance!"*

106-107 *"Because of you, I'll close my heart, and make myself suspicious of everything I see."*

swoons = faints
wherefore = why

Rats. Now my dress will crease.

117-119 *"Don't take away this heavy blow, fate! Death is the best way to hide her shame that we can hope for."*

123-131 *"Can she deny the story that her blushes have already proved? Don't live, Hero, don't open your eyes, for if I thought you were not about to die, if I thought your will to live was stronger than your sense of shame, I would kill you myself, not caring what other people thought. Was I upset that I had only one child? Did I complain at nature for not being more generous? Oh, you are one child too many!"*

133-134 *"Why didn't I adopt a homeless kid instead?"*

issue = child

Act 4, Scene 1

136-137 *"It's not my doing — this shame has been caused by an unkown father."*

Who smirched thus and mired with infamy, 135
I might have said "No part of it is mine —
This shame derives itself from unknown loins"?
But mine and mine I loved and mine I praised
And mine that I was proud on, mine so much
That I myself was to myself not mine, 140
Valuing of her — why, she, O, she is fallen
Into a pit of ink, that the wide sea
Hath drops too few to wash her clean again,
And salt too little which may season give
To her foul-tainted flesh!

BENEDICK   Sir, sir, be patient. 145
For my part, I am so attired in wonder,
I know not what to say.

attired in wonder = amazed

BEATRICE   O, on my soul, my cousin is belied!

belied = falsely accused

149 *"Beatrice, did you sleep in Hero's room last night?"*

BENEDICK   Lady, were you her bedfellow last night?

BEATRICE   No, truly not, although, until last night, 150
I have this twelvemonth been her bedfellow.

twelvemonth = year

152-153 *"It's proven! The case was strong as iron before, and now it's even stronger!"*

LEONATO   Confirmed, confirmed! O, that is stronger made
Which was before barred up with ribs of iron!
Would the two princes lie, and Claudio lie,
Who loved her so, that, speaking of her foulness, 155
Washed it with tears? Hence from her! Let her die.

157-160 *"Listen to me for a moment, I've only been quiet this long and let events run their course, because I was observing Hero."*

FRIAR FRANCIS   Hear me a little;
For I have only been silent so long,
And given way unto this course of fortune,
By noting of the lady. I have marked 160
A thousand blushing apparitions
To start into her face, a thousand innocent shames
In angel whiteness beat away those blushes,
And in her eye there hath appeared a fire,
To burn the errors that these princes hold 165
Against her maiden truth. Call me a fool;
Trust not my reading nor my observations,
Which with experimental seal doth warrant
The tenor of my book; trust not my age,
My reverence, calling, nor divinity, 170
If this sweet lady lie not guiltless here
Under some biting error.

166-172 *The Friar thinks Hero is innocent, and is willing to stake his reputation on it.*

LEONATO   Friar, it cannot be.
Thou seest that all the grace that she hath left
Is that she will not add to her damnation
A sin of perjury: she not denies it. 175
Why seek'st thou then to cover with excuse
That which appears in proper nakedness?

172-177 *"Friar, that can't be true. The only thing in her favour is that she's not denying it. So why are you trying to cover up the naked truth with excuses?"*

FRIAR FRANCIS   Lady, what man is he you are accused
of?

178-179 *"Lady, who's this man they accuse you of seeing?"*

HERO   They know that do accuse me; I know none. 180
If I know more of any man alive
Than that which maiden modesty doth warrant,
Let all my sins lack mercy! O my father,
Prove you that any man with me conversed
At hours unmeet, or that I yesternight 185

181-183 *"If I know more of any man alive than a modest virgin should, then let me be damned!"*

184-185 *"prove that any man spoke with me at an unsuitable hour"*

Maintained the change of words with any creature,
Refuse me, hate me, torture me to death!

FRIAR FRANCIS   There is some strange misprision in the
princes.

BENEDICK   Two of them have the very bent of honour,   190
And if their wisdoms be misled in this,
The practice of it lives in John the bastard,
Whose spirits toil in frame of villainies.

LEONATO   I know not. If they speak but truth of her,
These hands shall tear her. If they wrong her honour,   195
The proudest of them shall well hear of it.
Time hath not yet so dried this blood of mine,
Nor age so eat up my invention,
Nor fortune made such havoc of my means,
Nor my bad life reft me so much of friends,   200
But they shall find, awaked in such a kind,
Both strength of limb and policy of mind,
Ability in means and choice of friends,
To quit me of them throughly.

FRIAR FRANCIS   Pause awhile,
And let my counsel sway you in this case.   205
Your daughter here the princes left for dead,
Let her awhile be secretly kept in,
And publish it that she is dead indeed;
Maintain a mourning ostentation
And on your family's old monument   210
Hang mournful epitaphs and do all rites
That appertain unto a burial.

LEONATO   What shall become of this? What will this do?

FRIAR FRANCIS   Marry, this well carried shall on her behalf
Change slander to remorse — that is some good —   215
But not for that dream I on this strange course,
But on this travail look for greater birth.
She dying, as it must so be maintained,
Upon the instant that she was accused,
Shall be lamented, pitied and excused   220
Of every hearer: for it so falls out
That what we have we prize not to the worth
Whiles we enjoy it, but being lacked and lost,
Why, then we rack the value, then we find
The virtue that possession would not show us   225
Whiles it was ours. So will it fare with Claudio.
When he shall hear she died upon his words,
The idea of her life shall sweetly creep
Into his study of imagination,
And every lovely organ of her life   230
Shall come apparelled in more precious habit,
More moving-delicate and full of life,
Into the eye and prospect of his soul,
Than when she lived indeed. Then shall he mourn,
If ever love had interest in his liver,   235
And wish he had not so accused her,
No, though he thought his accusation true.
Let this be so, and doubt not but success

---

maintained the change of words =
exchanged words

misprision = misunderstanding

190-193 "Two of them are honourable
men, and if they have been deceived it
was the doing of Don John, who is
always working on some evil plan."

invention = mental powers

199 "nor has fortune so
destroyed my wealth"

reft = deprived

policy of mind = clear thinking

204 "to have my full revenge on them"

204-205 "Hold on a minute, and
let me give you some advice."

207-212 "Keep her at home, in
secret, for a while, and announce that
she really is dead, pretend to mourn,
and hang an epitaph on the family
tomb, and carry out a fake funeral."

214-217 "We'll change the nasty
accusations for sorrow — which is
something — but that's not my main
reason for coming up with this strange
plan, I'm hoping for an even better
result."

218-226 "The fact that she died,
according to our story, at the very instant
she was accused, will make everyone who
hears of it pity her. We don't value what
we have while we have it — only when it's
lost and gone do we see the goodness
that we ignored when we had it. That's
how it will be with Claudio."

230-231 "and everything that was
lovely about her in life will seem even
more precious"

234-235 "Then, if he has ever had
true feelings of love, he will mourn"

48

241-246 *"But even if the whole plan comes to nothing, at least her supposed death will distract people from the scandal. If the plan doesn't work, you can hide her in a convent."*

248-251 *"Take the friar's advice, and though you know how close I am to Don Pedro and Claudio, I swear I will help carry out this plan."*

253-254 *"I'm so upset, I'll do whatever I'm told."*

consented = agreed

256 *"There are strange remedies for strange illnesses."*

Benedick and Beatrice are left alone — they admit they love each other. Beatrice asks Benedick to kill Claudio. He's not very keen to murder his friend, but agrees to challenge him to a duel for Beatrice.

264-265 *"The man who saved her reputation would deserve so much from me!"*

even = straightforward

269 *"It's a job for a man, but not for you."*

277 *"Don't swear to something and then take it back."*

285-286 *"You've stopped me just at the right moment. I was about to announce that I loved you."*

Will fashion the event in better shape
Than I can lay it down in likelihood. 240
But if all aim but this be levelled false,
The supposition of the lady's death
Will quench the wonder of her infamy.
And if it sort not well, you may conceal her,
As best befits her wounded reputation, 245
In some reclusive and religious life,
Out of all eyes, tongues, minds and injuries.

BENEDICK Signior Leonato, let the friar advise you,
And though you know my inwardness and love
Is very much unto the Prince and Claudio, 250
Yet, by mine honour, I will deal in this
As secretly and justly as your soul
Should with your body.

LEONATO Being that I flow in grief,
The smallest twine may lead me.

FRIAR FRANCIS 'Tis well consented. Presently away; 255
For to strange sores strangely they strain the cure.
Come, lady, die to live. This wedding-day
Perhaps is but prolonged. Have patience and endure.

Exeunt all but BENEDICK and BEATRICE

BENEDICK Lady Beatrice, have you wept all this while?
BEATRICE Yea, and I will weep a while longer. 260
BENEDICK I will not desire that.
BEATRICE You have no reason — I do it freely.
BENEDICK Surely I do believe your fair cousin is wronged.
BEATRICE Ah, how much might the man deserve of me
that would right her! 265
BENEDICK Is there any way to show such friendship?
BEATRICE A very even way, but no such friend.
BENEDICK May a man do it?
BEATRICE It is a man's office, but not yours.
BENEDICK I do love nothing in the world so well as you: is 270
not that strange?
BEATRICE As strange as the thing I know not. It were as
possible for me to say I loved nothing so well as you.
But believe me not; and yet I lie not. I confess nothing,
nor I deny nothing. I am sorry for my cousin. 275
BENEDICK By my sword, Beatrice, thou lovest me.
BEATRICE Do not swear and eat it.
BENEDICK I will swear by it that you love me, and I will
make him eat it that says I love not you.
BEATRICE Will you not eat your word? 280
BENEDICK With no sauce that can be devised to it.
I protest I love thee.
BEATRICE Why, then, God forgive me!
BENEDICK What offence, sweet Beatrice?
BEATRICE You have stayed me in a happy hour. I was 285
about to protest I loved you.

Act 4, Scene 1

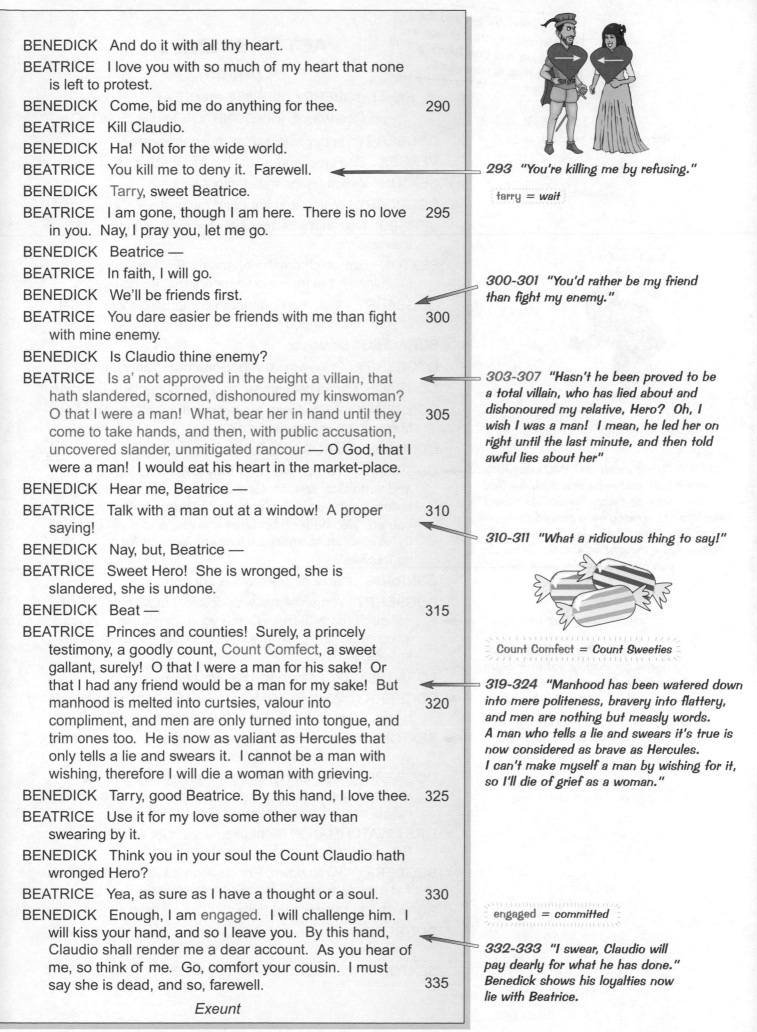

BENEDICK   And do it with all thy heart.

BEATRICE   I love you with so much of my heart that none is left to protest.

BENEDICK   Come, bid me do anything for thee.   290

BEATRICE   Kill Claudio.

BENEDICK   Ha! Not for the wide world.

BEATRICE   You kill me to deny it. Farewell.

293 "You're killing me by refusing."

BENEDICK   Tarry, sweet Beatrice.

tarry = wait

BEATRICE   I am gone, though I am here. There is no love   295
in you. Nay, I pray you, let me go.

BENEDICK   Beatrice —

BEATRICE   In faith, I will go.

BENEDICK   We'll be friends first.

300-301 "You'd rather be my friend than fight my enemy."

BEATRICE   You dare easier be friends with me than fight   300
with mine enemy.

BENEDICK   Is Claudio thine enemy?

BEATRICE   Is a' not approved in the height a villain, that
hath slandered, scorned, dishonoured my kinswoman?
O that I were a man! What, bear her in hand until they   305
come to take hands, and then, with public accusation,
uncovered slander, unmitigated rancour — O God, that I
were a man! I would eat his heart in the market-place.

303-307 "Hasn't he been proved to be a total villain, who has lied about and dishonoured my relative, Hero? Oh, I wish I was a man! I mean, he led her on right until the last minute, and then told awful lies about her"

BENEDICK   Hear me, Beatrice —

BEATRICE   Talk with a man out at a window! A proper   310
saying!

310-311 "What a ridiculous thing to say!"

BENEDICK   Nay, but, Beatrice —

BEATRICE   Sweet Hero! She is wronged, she is
slandered, she is undone.

BENEDICK   Beat —   315

BEATRICE   Princes and counties! Surely, a princely
testimony, a goodly count, Count Comfect, a sweet
gallant, surely! O that I were a man for his sake! Or
that I had any friend would be a man for my sake! But
manhood is melted into curtsies, valour into   320
compliment, and men are only turned into tongue, and
trim ones too. He is now as valiant as Hercules that
only tells a lie and swears it. I cannot be a man with
wishing, therefore I will die a woman with grieving.

Count Comfect = Count Sweeties

319-324 "Manhood has been watered down into mere politeness, bravery into flattery, and men are nothing but measly words.
A man who tells a lie and swears it's true is now considered as brave as Hercules.
I can't make myself a man by wishing for it, so I'll die of grief as a woman."

BENEDICK   Tarry, good Beatrice. By this hand, I love thee.   325

BEATRICE   Use it for my love some other way than
swearing by it.

BENEDICK   Think you in your soul the Count Claudio hath
wronged Hero?

BEATRICE   Yea, as sure as I have a thought or a soul.   330

engaged = committed

BENEDICK   Enough, I am engaged. I will challenge him. I
will kiss your hand, and so I leave you. By this hand,
Claudio shall render me a dear account. As you hear of
me, so think of me. Go, comfort your cousin. I must
say she is dead, and so, farewell.   335

332-333 "I swear, Claudio will pay dearly for what he has done."
Benedick shows his loyalties now lie with Beatrice.

Exeunt

Act 4, Scene 1

50

Dogberry, Verges and the Sexton interrogate Conrade and Borachio and Don John's evil plotting is unmasked...

ACT 4 SCENE 2
A prison

Enter DOGBERRY, VERGES and SEXTON in gowns,
and the Watch, with CONRADE and BORACHIO

DOGBERRY Is our whole dissembly appeared?

VERGES O, a stool and a cushion for the Sexton.

SEXTON Which be the malefactors?

DOGBERRY Marry, that am I and my partner.

VERGES Nay, that's certain. We have the exhibition to examine. 5

SEXTON But which are the offenders that are to be examined? Let them come before master constable.

DOGBERRY Yea, marry, let them come before me. What is your name, friend? 10

BORACHIO Borachio.

DOGBERRY Pray, write down, Borachio. Yours, sirrah?

CONRADE I am a gentleman, sir, and my name is Conrade.

DOGBERRY Write down, master gentleman Conrade. Masters, do you serve God? 15

CONRADE *and* BORACHIO Yea, sir, we hope.

DOGBERRY Write down, that they hope they serve God, and write God first, for God defend but God should go before such villains! Masters, it is proved already that you are little better than false knaves, and it will go near 20 to be thought so shortly. How answer you for yourselves?

CONRADE Marry, sir, we say we are none.

DOGBERRY A marvellous witty fellow, I assure you, but I will go about with him. Come you hither, sirrah. A word 25 in your ear. Sir, I say to you, it is thought you are false knaves.

BORACHIO Sir, I say to you we are none.

DOGBERRY Well, stand aside. 'Fore God, they are both in a tale. Have you writ down that they are none? 30

SEXTON Master constable, you go not the way to examine. You must call forth the Watch that are their accusers.

DOGBERRY Yea, marry, that's the eftest way. Let the Watch come forth. Masters, I charge you, in the Prince's name, accuse these men. 35

FIRST WATCHMAN This man said, sir, that Don John, the Prince's brother, was a villain.

DOGBERRY Write down, Prince John a villain. Why, this is flat perjury, to call a Prince's brother villain.

BORACHIO Master constable — 40

DOGBERRY Pray thee, fellow, peace. I do not like thy look, I promise thee.

SEXTON What heard you him say else?

---

dissembly = *he means 'assembly'*

Sexton = *churchyard handyman*

malefactors = *criminals*

Don't mind me. I'll stand.

sirrah = *boy*

17-22 *"Write down that they hope they serve God, and write God first, for God must go before rascals like these! Masters, it's already been proved that you are little better than lying hounds, and it will nearly be thought so shortly. What do you have to say for yourselves?"*

25 *"Deal with him."*

29-30 *"By God, it looks as though they've got their story straight. Have you written down that they're not lying hounds?"*

31-32 *"You're not questioning them right. You have to call the Watch who charged them."*

eftest = *a made up word, probably meaning 'best'*

Act 4, Scene 2

SECOND WATCHMAN   Marry, that he had received a thousand ducats of Don John for accusing the Lady Hero wrongfully.   45

DOGBERRY   Flat burglary as ever was committed.

VERGES   Yea, by mass, that it is.

SEXTON   What else, fellow?

FIRST WATCHMAN   And that Count Claudio did mean, upon his words, to disgrace Hero before the whole assembly, and not marry her.   50

DOGBERRY   O villain! Thou wilt be condemned into everlasting redemption for this.

SEXTON   What else?   55

WATCHMAN   This is all.

SEXTON   And this is more, masters, than you can deny. Prince John is this morning secretly stolen away. Hero was in this manner accused, in this very manner refused, and upon the grief of this suddenly died.   60 Master constable, let these men be bound, and brought to Leonato's. I will go before and show him their examination.

Exit

DOGBERRY   Come, let them be opinioned.

VERGES   Let them be in the hands —   65

CONRADE   Off, coxcomb!

DOGBERRY   God's my life, where's the sexton? Let him write down, the Prince's officer coxcomb. Come, bind them. Thou naughty varlet!

CONRADE   Away! You are an ass, you are an ass.   70

DOGBERRY   Dost thou not suspect my place? Dost thou not suspect my years? O that he were here to write me down an ass! But, masters, remember that I am an ass — though it be not written down, yet forget not that I am an ass. No, thou villain, thou art full of piety, as shall be   75 proved upon thee by good witness. I am a wise fellow, and, which is more, an officer, and, which is more, a householder, and, which is more, as pretty a piece of flesh as any is in Messina, and one that knows the law, go to; and a rich fellow enough, go to; and a fellow that   80 hath had losses, and one that hath two gowns and everything handsome about him. Bring him away. O that I had been writ down an ass!

Exeunt

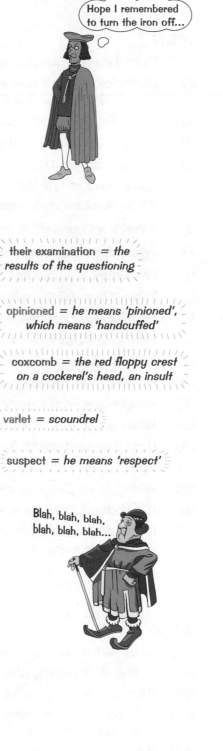

44-46 *"Well, that Don John had given him a thousand ducats for falsely accusing Hero."*

Hope I remembered to turn the iron off...

their examination = *the results of the questioning*

opinioned = *he means 'pinioned', which means 'handcuffed'*

coxcomb = *the red floppy crest on a cockerel's head, an insult*

varlet = *scoundrel*

suspect = *he means 'respect'*

Blah, blah, blah, blah, blah, blah...

Act 4, Scene 2

Act 4 — Revision Summary

The fourth delightful Revision Summary in our series of five, sports a fantastic 28 questions, genuine leatherette quotation marks and an easy-clean hob. Sink back in a comfortable chair and soak up the seductive aroma of a helpful revision aid. Don't just take our word for it: "Kicks butt." — W. Shakespeare. "The best we've seen." — Official Which? Page 52 Guide.

SCENE 1

1) Does Leonato want a long drawn-out ceremony or a short 'n' sweet one?

2) Benedick doesn't understand why Claudio's being so moody and tries to lighten the mood. Write out the lines where he does this in full.

3) What fruit does Claudio compare Hero to? What does he mean by his comparison?

4) In lines 33 to 42, does Claudio think Hero is blushing because she's guilty or innocent?

5) In lines 46 to 48 Leonato says to Claudio: "Dear my lord, if you, in your own proof,/ Have vanquished the resistance of her youth,/ And made defeat of her virginity —". What does he think has happened?

6) What's a "nuptial"?

7) What does Don Pedro think of Hero?

8) Who does Claudio call "most foul, most fair"? What does he mean?

9) When Hero faints, who says he thinks it would be best if she died?

10) Who <u>doesn't</u> believe the story about Hero straightaway? Name three characters.

11) Why can't Beatrice prove that the story about Hero is made up?

12) Who first suggests Don John has been playing rotten tricks?

13) Explain Friar Francis's plan in your own words.

14) What does Friar Francis think the effect of his plan will be on Claudio?

15) What does Friar Francis suggest Hero can do if the plan doesn't work out?

16) Does Leonato agree to the plan?

17) Write down Benedick's exact words when he tells Beatrice he loves her.

18) Write down Beatrice's exact words when she admits she loves Benedick.

19) What does Beatrice ask Benedick to do to prove he loves her?

20) Write down a phrase from Beatrice's speech in lines 316-324 that shows she thinks Benedick's being a wimp.

21) At the end of the scene, Benedick says, "By this hand, Claudio shall render me a dear account." Write this down in your own words.

SCENE 2

22) What word does Dogberry use to mean "assembly"?

23) In line 4 Dogberry claims to be a "malefactor". Explain why he's wrong.

24) Who are being questioned in this scene? Name two characters.

25) In lines 31-32 the Sexton tells Dogberry he's doing his investigation all wrong. What does the Sexton say he should do?

26) Who goes to tell Leonato what has happened?

27) What's a coxcomb?

28) How does Dogberry feel about being called an ass?

ACT 5 SCENE 1
Before Leonato's house

Enter LEONATO *and* ANTONIO

Antonio advises Leonato not to be so upset but he won't listen. Antonio and Leonato nearly fight Don Pedro and Claudio, then Benedick challenges Claudio to a duel. Dogberry arrives with Borachio and the plot to ruin Hero and Claudio's wedding is revealed at last.

ANTONIO   If you go on thus, you will kill yourself,
    And 'tis not wisdom thus to second grief
    Against yourself.

2-3 "it's not wise to turn your grief against yourself."

LEONATO   I pray thee, cease thy counsel,
    Which falls into mine ears as profitless
    As water in a sieve. Give not me counsel,   5
    Nor let no comforter delight mine ear
    But such a one whose wrongs do suit with mine.
    Bring me a father that so loved his child,
    Whose joy of her is overwhelmed like mine,
    And bid him speak of patience;   10
    Measure his woe the length and breadth of mine
    And let it answer every strain for strain,
    As thus for thus and such a grief for such,
    In every lineament, branch, shape, and form.
    If such a one will smile and stroke his beard,   15
    Bid sorrow wag, cry "hem!" when he should groan,
    Patch grief with proverbs, make misfortune drunk
    With candle-wasters; bring him yet to me,
    And I of him will gather patience.
    But there is no such man: for, brother, men   20
    Can counsel and speak comfort to that grief
    Which they themselves not feel; but, tasting it,
    Their counsel turns to passion, which before
    Would give preceptial medicine to rage,
    Fetter strong madness in a silken thread,   25
    Charm ache with air and agony with words.
    No, no, 'tis all men's office to speak patience
    To those that wring under the load of sorrow,
    But no man's virtue nor sufficiency
    To be so moral when he shall endure   30
    The like himself. Therefore give me no counsel.
    My griefs cry louder than advertisement.

3-5 "Please stop giving me advice — it sticks in my ears no better than water in a sieve."

8-12 "Bring me a father who loved his child as much as me, whose delight in her has been overturned like mine, and __he__ can tell me to control myself. And make sure he's been hurt just as much as me."

answer = match

15-19 "If that man will smile and stroke his beard, tell me to ignore my sorrow, say "Ahem!" when he should be groaning, offer proverbs as comfort for grief, drug my sorrow with second-rate philosophy — you can bring him to me, and I'll accept his advice to control myself."

20-26 "Men can only give advice and comfort for problems they don't have personal experience of. Once they experience the problem personally they start being all emotional about it, whereas before they'd think everything could be sorted out with words."

27-31 "No, no, it's the way of all men to advise those who suffer sorrow to be calm, but no man's so virtuous that he can go through the same himself."

advertisement = advice

ANTONIO   Therein do men from children nothing differ.

LEONATO   I pray thee, peace. I will be flesh and blood;
    For there was never yet philosopher   35
    That could endure the toothache patiently,
    However they have writ the style of gods
    And made a push at chance and sufferance.

35-38 "There has never been a philosopher who could calmly put up with a toothache, however much his writings advised behaving in the manner of gods, and scoffed at chance and suffering."

ANTONIO   Yet bend not all the harm upon yourself;
    Make those that do offend you suffer too.   40

LEONATO   There thou speak'st reason. Nay, I will do so.
    My soul doth tell me Hero is belied;
    And that shall Claudio know; so shall the Prince
    And all of them that thus dishonour her.

ANTONIO   Here comes the Prince and Claudio hastily.   45

Enter DON PEDRO *and* CLAUDIO

DON PEDRO   Good den, good den.

CLAUDIO   Good day to both of you.

Aspirin, please.

42 "I know in my heart that Hero has been falsely accused"

48 "We're in a hurry, Leonato."

Me? Touching my sword? Nah...

dissembler = liar

56-58 "Damn my hand, if it has frightened an old gent like you. I promise you, I didn't mean anything by putting my hand on my sword."

fleer = sneer

60-67 "I'm not speaking like some doddery old man, who has an excuse to brag about what he did when he was young, or what he would do if he was not old. Stick this between your ears, Claudio — you have so insulted my innocent child and me that I am forced to set aside the dignity of my old age, and challenge you to a duel."

75-77 "I'll prove it in a fight if he dares to take up the challenge, despite his fancy fencing skills and his training, his youth and his strength."

daff = dismiss

83 "beat me in a fight and I'm all yours"

foining fence = style of sword-fighting where you knock away the other person's blows instead of trying to stab at them — Antonio's saying he wants a proper fight.

89-91 "Her death caused by the lies of scoundrels who are as likely to accept my challenge to a fight as I am to take a snake by the tongue."

LEONATO Hear you, my lords —

DON PEDRO We have some haste, Leonato.

LEONATO Some haste, my lord! Well, fare you well, my lord!
  Are you so hasty now? Well, all is one.   50

DON PEDRO Nay, do not quarrel with us, good old man.

ANTONIO If he could right himself with quarrelling,
  Some of us would lie low.

CLAUDIO   Who wrongs him?

LEONATO Marry, thou dost wrong me, thou dissembler,
                              thou —
  Nay, never lay thy hand upon thy sword;   55
  I fear thee not.

CLAUDIO   Marry, beshrew my hand
  If it should give your age such cause of fear.
  In faith, my hand meant nothing to my sword.

LEONATO Tush, tush, man, never fleer and jest at me!
  I speak not like a dotard nor a fool,   60
  As under privilege of age to brag
  What I have done being young, or what would do
  Were I not old. Know, Claudio, to thy head,
  Thou hast so wronged mine innocent child and me
  That I am forced to lay my reverence by   65
  And, with grey hairs and bruise of many days,
  Do challenge thee to trial of a man.
  I say thou hast belied mine innocent child.
  Thy slander hath gone through and through her heart,
  And she lies buried with her ancestors —   70
  O, in a tomb where never scandal slept,
  Save this of hers, framed by thy villainy!

CLAUDIO My villainy?

LEONATO   Thine, Claudio; thine, I say.

DON PEDRO You say not right, old man.

LEONATO   My lord, my lord,
  I'll prove it on his body, if he dare,   75
  Despite his nice fence and his active practice,
  His May of youth and bloom of lustihood.

CLAUDIO Away! I will not have to do with you.

LEONATO Canst thou so daff me? Thou hast killed my child.
  If thou kill'st me, boy, thou shalt kill a man.   80

ANTONIO He shall kill two of us, and men indeed.
  But that's no matter, let him kill one first.
  Win me and wear me, let him answer me.
  Come, follow me, boy. Come, sir boy, come, follow me.
  Sir boy, I'll whip you from your foining fence!   85
  Nay, as I am a gentleman, I will.

LEONATO Brother —

ANTONIO Content yourself. God knows I loved my niece,
  And she is dead, slandered to death by villains,
  That dare as well answer a man indeed   90
  As I dare take a serpent by the tongue.
  Boys, apes, braggarts, Jacks, milksops!

LEONATO   Brother Antony —

ANTONIO   Hold you content. What, man! I know them, yea,
And what they weigh, even to the utmost scruple. 95
Scambling, out-facing, fashion-monging boys,
That lie and cog and flout, deprave and slander,
Go anticly, show outward hideousness,
And speak off half a dozen dangerous words,
How they might hurt their enemies, if they durst — 100
And this is all.

LEONATO   But, brother Antony —

ANTONIO   Come, 'tis no matter.
Do not you meddle; let me deal in this.

DON PEDRO   Gentlemen both, we will not wake your
                                         patience.
My heart is sorry for your daughter's death, 105
But, on my honour, she was charged with nothing
But what was true and very full of proof.

LEONATO   My lord, my lord —

DON PEDRO   I will not hear you.

LEONATO   No? Come, brother; away! I will be heard. 110

ANTONIO   And shall, or some of us will smart for it.

            Exeunt LEONATO *and* ANTONIO

DON PEDRO   See, see! Here comes the man we went to
seek.

            Enter BENEDICK

CLAUDIO   Now, signior, what news?

BENEDICK   Good day, my lord. 115

DON PEDRO   Welcome, signior. You are almost come to
part almost a fray.

CLAUDIO   We had like to have had our two noses snapped
off with two old men without teeth.

DON PEDRO   Leonato and his brother. What thinkest 120
thou? Had we fought, I doubt we should have been too
young for them.

BENEDICK   In a false quarrel there is no true valour. I
came to seek you both.

CLAUDIO   We have been up and down to seek thee, for we 125
are high-proof melancholy and would fain have it
beaten away. Wilt thou use thy wit?

BENEDICK   It is in my scabbard — shall I draw it?

DON PEDRO   Dost thou wear thy wit by thy side?

CLAUDIO   Never any did so, though very many have been 130
beside their wit. I will bid thee draw, as we do the
minstrels — draw, to pleasure us.

DON PEDRO   As I am an honest man, he looks pale. Art
thou sick, or angry?

CLAUDIO   What, courage, man! What though care killed a 135
cat, thou hast mettle enough in thee to kill care.

94-100 "You stay out of it, old chap. I know their sort. Rough, competitive, fashion-following boys, who lie and cheat and mock, give others a bad name and behave like buffoons, babbling lots of threats about how they'd hurt their enemies, if they dared."

104-107 "Gentlemen, we won't test your patience. I'm really sorry for your daughter's death, but everything she was accused of was proved to be true."

smart = suffer

116-117 "You were almost in time to stop what was almost a fight."

118-119 "We almost had our noses bitten off by two toothless old men."

My dog's got no nose.

How does he smell?

Awful.

125-127 "We've been all over looking for you, because we're feeling sad, and would like to be cheered up. Will you say something funny?"

130-132 "Nobody has ever worn their wit by their side, though many have been beside themselves. I'm asking you to be funny in the same way I would ask a minstrel — to entertain us."

135-136 "Chin up, man! Sadness killed the cat, but you've got the guts to kill sadness."

137-138 "I shall have to cut your wit off in full flow if you use it against me."

BENEDICK Sir, I shall meet your wit in the career, and you charge it against me. I pray you choose another subject.

139-140 "Then give him another lance to fight with, the one he's got is broken."

CLAUDIO Nay, then, give him another staff; this last was broke cross.   140

DON PEDRO By this light, he changes more and more. I think he be angry indeed.

143 "If he's angry, he's ready to fight."

CLAUDIO If he be, he knows how to turn his girdle.

BENEDICK Shall I speak a word in your ear?

God bless me = God save me

CLAUDIO God bless me from a challenge!   145

146-149 "I'm not joking, I'll fight you over this however you like, with whatever weapons you dare to use and whatever time you dare to fight. You'll meet my challenge, or I'll call you a coward."

BENEDICK *(aside to Claudio)* You are a villain. I jest not; I will make it good how you dare, with what you dare, and when you dare. Do me right, or I will protest your cowardice. You have killed a sweet lady, and her death shall fall heavy on you. Let me hear from you.   150

151 "I'll fight you then. It'll be a laugh."

CLAUDIO Well, I will meet you, so I may have good cheer.

DON PEDRO What, a feast, a feast?

153-155 "I thank him — he's invited me to eat a calf's head and a chicken, and if I don't do an outstanding job of carving it you can say my knife's useless."

CLAUDIO I' faith, I thank him, he hath bid me to a calf's head and a capon, the which if I do not carve most curiously, say my knife's naught. Shall I not find a woodcock too?   155

woodcock = bird known for being easy to catch

BENEDICK Sir, your wit ambles well; it goes easily.

DON PEDRO I'll tell thee how Beatrice praised thy wit the other day. I said, thou hadst a fine wit: "True," said she, "a fine little one." "No," said I, "a great wit." "Right," says   160 she, "a great gross one." "Nay," said I, "a good wit." "Just," said she, "it hurts nobody." "Nay," said I, "the gentleman is wise." "Certain," said she, "a wise

just = fair enough

164-167 " 'No!' I said, 'he speaks several languages (tongues).' 'I can believe that,' she said, 'because he promised something to me on Monday night, and broke his promise on Tuesday morning — that's a double tongue for you.' "

gentleman." "Nay," said I, "he hath the tongues." "That I believe," said she, "for he swore a thing to me on   165 Monday night, which he forswore on Tuesday morning; there's a double tongue; there's two tongues." Thus did she, an hour together, transshape thy particular virtues. Yet at last she concluded with a sigh, thou wast the properest man in Italy.   170

CLAUDIO For the which she wept heartily and said she cared not.

transshape = transform, misdescribe

properest = finest

DON PEDRO Yea, that she did: but yet, for all that, an if she did not hate him deadly, she would love him dearly — the old man's daughter told us all.   175

CLAUDIO All, all — and, moreover, God saw him when he was hid in the garden.

178-179 "But when will we see Benedick married?" It's the old gag about a married man having horns on his head as a sign that his wife's being unfaithful.

DON PEDRO But when shall we set the savage bull's horns on the sensible Benedick's head?

CLAUDIO Yea, and text underneath, "Here dwells Benedick 180 the married man."

182-186 "So long, boy, you know what I think. I'll leave you to your gossipy jokes. You make jokes, like bragging fools who break their swordblades — neither of them hurts a bit, thank God. My lord, I thank you for your kind treatment. I can have nothing more to do with you."

BENEDICK Fare you well, boy, you know my mind. I will leave you now to your gossip-like humour. You break jests as braggarts do their blades, which God be thanked, hurt not. My lord, for your many courtesies I   185 thank you. I must discontinue your company. Your brother the bastard is fled from Messina. You have

Act 5, Scene 1

among you killed a sweet and innocent lady. For my
Lord Lackbeard there, he and I shall meet; and, till then,
peace be with him.   190

Exit

DON PEDRO   He is in earnest.

CLAUDIO   In most profound earnest; and, I'll warrant you,
for the love of Beatrice.

DON PEDRO   And hath challenged thee?

CLAUDIO   Most sincerely.   195

DON PEDRO   What a pretty thing man is when he goes in
his doublet and hose and leaves off his wit!

CLAUDIO   He is then a giant to an ape, but then is an ape
a doctor to such a man.

DON PEDRO   But, soft you, let me be! Pluck up, my heart,   200
and be sad. Did he not say, my brother was fled?

Enter DOGBERRY, VERGES *and the Watch,*
with CONRADE *and* BORACHIO

DOGBERRY   Come you, sir. If justice cannot tame you,
she shall ne'er weigh more reasons in her balance.
Nay, an you be a cursing hypocrite once, you must be
looked to.   205

DON PEDRO   How now? Two of my brother's men bound!
Borachio one!

CLAUDIO   Hearken after their offence, my lord.

DON PEDRO   Officers, what offence have these men
done?   210

DOGBERRY   Marry, sir, they have committed false report.
Moreover, they have spoken untruths; secondarily, they
are slanders; sixth and lastly, they have belied a lady;
thirdly, they have verified unjust things; and, to
conclude, they are lying knaves.   215

DON PEDRO   First, I ask thee what they have done; thirdly,
I ask thee what's their offence; sixth and lastly, why they
are committed; and, to conclude, what you lay to their
charge.

CLAUDIO   Rightly reasoned, and in his own division, and,   220
by my troth, there's one meaning well suited.

DON PEDRO   Who have you offended, masters, that you
are thus bound to your answer? This learned constable
is too cunning to be understood. What's your offence?

BORACHIO   Sweet Prince, let me go no farther to mine   225
answer, do you hear me, and let this count kill me. I
have deceived even your very eyes. What your wisdoms
could not discover, these shallow fools have brought to
light, who in the night overheard me confessing to this
man how Don John your brother incensed me to slander   230
the Lady Hero, how you were brought into the orchard
and saw me court Margaret in Hero's garments, how
you disgraced her, when you should marry her. My
villainy they have upon record, which I had rather seal

Lord Lackbeard =
Claudio, Benedick's
calling him immature

earnest = *serious*

warrant = *bet*

*196-197 "Doesn't a man look ridiculous
when he puts on his jacket and trousers
and forgets his common sense."*

*198-199 "A man who forgets his common
sense is like a giant ape, but then an ape
is as clever as a doctor compared to a
man like that."*

*200-201 "Shush a minute, let me
think! It's time to stop messing
around and be serious. Didn't he say
my brother has run away?"*

*202-205 "Come on. If justice can't
sort you out, she'll give up altogether.
Liars need to be dealt with."*

bound = *tied up*

*208 "Ask what they've
done wrong."*

*211-215 All different ways of
saying, "They've told lies."*

*216-219 All different ways of
saying, "What have they done?"*

*220-221 "Perfectly logical, in his
own style, and, I swear, there's
one meaning well disguised."*

too cunning = *Don Pedro's being
sarky — he means too confusing*

*225-226 "Don't make me answer, just
let Claudio kill me."*

incensed = *incited*

seal = *confirm*

58

235-237 "Hero's dead because Don John and I told lies about her, and, basically, I don't want anything except to be punished like the villain I am."

with my death than repeat over to my shame. The lady is dead upon mine and my master's false accusation, and, briefly, I desire nothing but the reward of a villain. **235**

238-239 "Don't his words make your blood run cold?"

DON PEDRO   Runs not this speech like iron through your blood?

240 "I feel like I've been poisoned."

CLAUDIO   I have drunk poison whiles he uttered it. **240**

241 "Did my brother make you do this?"

DON PEDRO   But did my brother set thee on to this?

BORACHIO   Yea, and paid me richly for the practice of it.

243-244 "He's a traitor through and through, and he's run off because all this evil is his doing."

DON PEDRO   He is composed and framed of treachery, And fled he is upon this villainy.

245-246 "Now I can see you as I did when I first loved you."

CLAUDIO   Sweet Hero! Now thy image doth appear In the rare semblance that I loved it first. **245**

plaintiffs = accused men

reformed = he means 'informed'

DOGBERRY   Come, bring away the plaintiffs. By this time our sexton hath reformed Signior Leonato of the matter. And, masters, do not forget to specify, when time and place shall serve, that I am an ass. **250**

249-250 "when the time and place are right, do not forget to make it clear that I am an ass."

VERGES   Here, here comes master Signior Leonato, and the Sexton too.

Blah, blah, blah, blah, blah, blah... note = notice

Re-enter LEONATO and ANTONIO with the SEXTON

LEONATO   Which is the villain? Let me see his eyes, That, when I note another man like him, I may avoid him. Which of these is he? **255**

thy breath = your words

BORACHIO   If you would know your wronger, look on me.

LEONATO   Art thou the slave that with thy breath hast killed Mine innocent child?

BORACHIO   Yea, even I alone.

260-262 "No, not quite, villain — you're too hard on yourself. Here's another pair of (dis)honourable men — a third, who was also involved, has fled." I.e. Claudio and Don Pedro are responsible too.

LEONATO   No, not so, villain — thou beliest thyself. Here stand a pair of honourable men, A third is fled, that had a hand in it. I thank you, princes, for my daughter's death. Record it with your high and worthy deeds. 'Twas bravely done, if you bethink you of it. **260** **265**

266-270 "I don't know how to ask you to hear me out, but I must speak. Choose your revenge yourself — force me to take whatever punishment you can come up with for my wrong-doing. But the only thing I did wrong was to make a mistake."

CLAUDIO   I know not how to pray your patience, Yet I must speak. Choose your revenge yourself; Impose me to what penance your invention Can lay upon my sin. Yet sinned I not But in mistaking.

DON PEDRO   By my soul, nor I; And yet, to satisfy this good old man, I would bend under any heavy weight That he'll enjoin me to. **270**

enjoin me to = lay upon me

274-280 "I can't tell you to tell my daughter to come back to life — that's impossible — but I do ask you both to tell the people of Messina that she died innocent, and if you can do this, make an inscription for her tomb, and sing it to her bones tonight."

LEONATO   I cannot bid you bid my daughter live — That were impossible — but, I pray you both, Possess the people in Messina here How innocent she died, and if your love Can labour ought in sad invention, Hang her an epitaph upon her tomb And sing it to her bones, sing it to-night. Tomorrow morning come you to my house, And since you could not be my son-in-law, Be yet my nephew. My brother hath a daughter, **275** **280**

Act 5, Scene 1

Almost the copy of my child that's dead,
And she alone is heir to both of us.   285
Give her the right you should have given her cousin,
And so dies my revenge.

CLAUDIO   O noble sir,
Your over-kindness doth wring tears from me!
I do embrace your offer; and dispose
For henceforth of poor Claudio.   290

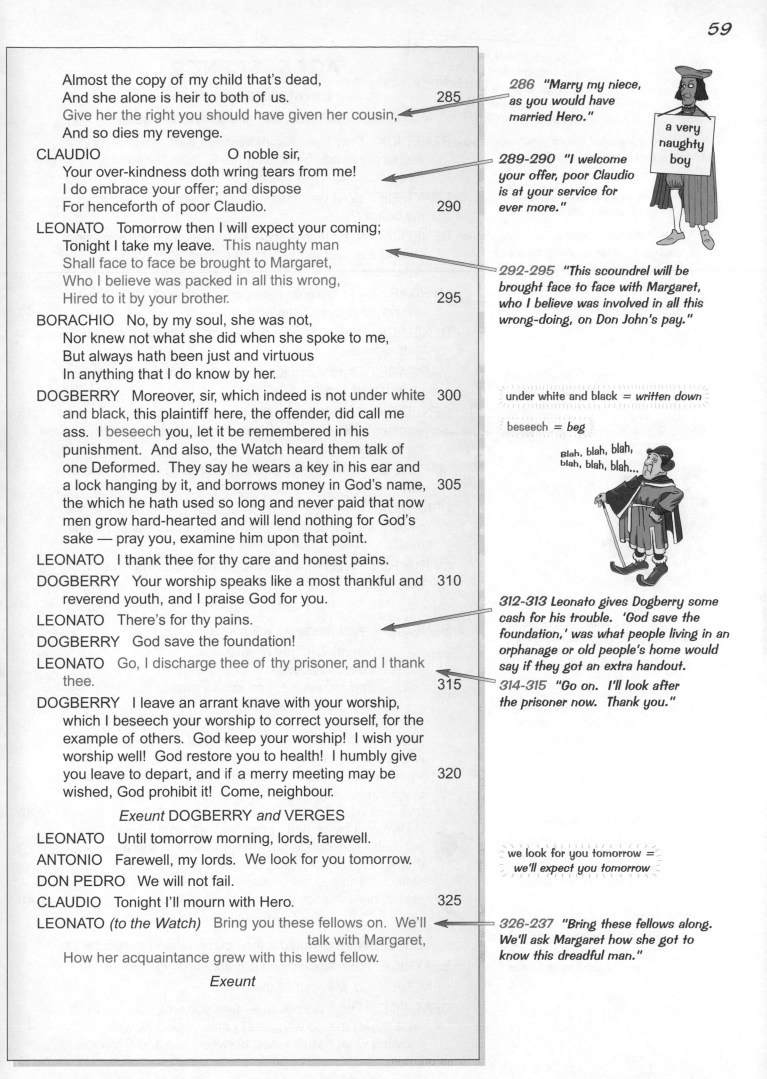

286 "Marry my niece, as you would have married Hero."

a very naughty boy

289-290 "I welcome your offer, poor Claudio is at your service for ever more."

LEONATO Tomorrow then I will expect your coming;
Tonight I take my leave. This naughty man
Shall face to face be brought to Margaret,
Who I believe was packed in all this wrong,
Hired to it by your brother.   295

292-295 "This scoundrel will be brought face to face with Margaret, who I believe was involved in all this wrong-doing, on Don John's pay."

BORACHIO No, by my soul, she was not,
Nor knew not what she did when she spoke to me,
But always hath been just and virtuous
In anything that I do know by her.

DOGBERRY Moreover, sir, which indeed is not under white   300
and black, this plaintiff here, the offender, did call me
ass. I beseech you, let it be remembered in his
punishment. And also, the Watch heard them talk of
one Deformed. They say he wears a key in his ear and
a lock hanging by it, and borrows money in God's name,   305
the which he hath used so long and never paid that now
men grow hard-hearted and will lend nothing for God's
sake — pray you, examine him upon that point.

under white and black = written down

beseech = beg

Blah, blah, blah, blah, blah, blah...

LEONATO I thank thee for thy care and honest pains.

DOGBERRY Your worship speaks like a most thankful and   310
reverend youth, and I praise God for you.

LEONATO There's for thy pains.

DOGBERRY God save the foundation!

312-313 Leonato gives Dogberry some cash for his trouble. 'God save the foundation,' was what people living in an orphanage or old people's home would say if they got an extra handout.

LEONATO Go, I discharge thee of thy prisoner, and I thank
thee.   315

314-315 "Go on. I'll look after the prisoner now. Thank you."

DOGBERRY I leave an arrant knave with your worship,
which I beseech your worship to correct yourself, for the
example of others. God keep your worship! I wish your
worship well! God restore you to health! I humbly give
you leave to depart, and if a merry meeting may be   320
wished, God prohibit it! Come, neighbour.

        Exeunt DOGBERRY *and* VERGES

LEONATO Until tomorrow morning, lords, farewell.

ANTONIO Farewell, my lords. We look for you tomorrow.

DON PEDRO We will not fail.

we look for you tomorrow = we'll expect you tomorrow

CLAUDIO Tonight I'll mourn with Hero.   325

LEONATO *(to the Watch)* Bring you these fellows on. We'll
                        talk with Margaret,
How her acquaintance grew with this lewd fellow.

326-237 "Bring these fellows along. We'll ask Margaret how she got to know this dreadful man."

        Exeunt

Act 5, Scene 1

Benedick and Beatrice meet in Leonato's garden and have a jokey (but basically lovey-dovey) chat.

ACT 5   SCENE 2
Leonato's garden

Enter BENEDICK *and* MARGARET, *meeting*

1-3 *"Do me a massive favour, and help me have a conversation with Beatrice."*

BENEDICK   Pray thee, sweet Mistress Margaret, deserve well at my hands by helping me to the speech of Beatrice.

sonnet = *type of rhyming poem with 14 lines*

MARGARET   Will you then write me a sonnet in praise of my beauty?   5

6-8 *"It'll be in such a fine style, Margaret, that no living man will outdo it, because, it's got to be said, you're worth it."*

BENEDICK   In so high a style, Margaret, that no man living shall come over it, for, in most comely truth, thou deservest it.

9-10 *"What, will I always be a servant?"*

MARGARET   To have no man come over me! Why, shall I always keep below stairs?   10

BENEDICK   Thy wit is as quick as the greyhound's mouth — it catches.

fencer's foils = *blunt swords for practising*

MARGARET   And yours as blunt as the fencer's foils, which hit, but hurt not.

16-17 *"I give in — have the shields."*

BENEDICK   A most manly wit, Margaret — it will not hurt a woman. And so, I pray thee, call Beatrice. I give thee the bucklers.   15

Yours looks like a Rolo.

MARGARET   Give us the swords; we have bucklers of our own.

pikes = *spikes*

BENEDICK   If you use them, Margaret, you must put in the pikes with a vice, and they are dangerous weapons for maids.   20

MARGARET   Well, I will call Beatrice to you, who I think hath legs.

Exit MARGARET

BENEDICK   And therefore will come.   25

(sings) *The god of love,*
That sits above,
And knows me, and knows me,
How pitiful I deserve —

Leander = *character from Greek mythology who drowned swimming across the sea between Greece and Turkey to see his girlfriend Hero*

Troilus, panders = *Troilus was another chap from Greek mythology, a Trojan who fell in love with a Greek girl. His Uncle Pandarus was their go-between.*

quondam carpet-mongers = *people who used to frequent women's bedrooms — where the floors were carpeted.*

blank verse = *non-rhyming poetry used to tell a story, like the poetry bits of Much Ado*

ominous = *bad*

39-40 *"I wasn't born to be a good rhymer, and I can't be a light-hearted lover."*

I mean in singing — but in loving, Leander the good   30
swimmer, Troilus the first employer of panders, and a whole bookful of these quondam carpet-mongers, whose names yet run smoothly in the even road of a blank verse, why, they were never so truly turned over and over as my poor self in love. Marry, I cannot show it   35
in rhyme. I have tried. I can find out no rhyme to 'lady' but 'baby', an innocent rhyme; for 'scorn', 'horn', a hard rhyme; for 'school', 'fool', a babbling rhyme; very ominous endings. No, I was not born under a rhyming planet, nor I cannot woo in festival terms.   40

Enter BEATRICE

Sweet Beatrice, wouldst thou come when I called thee?

BEATRICE   Yea, signior, and depart when you bid me.

BENEDICK   O, stay but till then!

BEATRICE   'Then' is spoken — fare you well now, and yet, ere I go, let me go with that I came, which is, with   45
knowing what hath passed between you and Claudio.

BENEDICK Only foul words; and thereupon I will kiss thee.

BEATRICE Foul words is but foul wind, and foul wind is but foul breath, and foul breath is noisome — therefore I will depart unkissed. 50

noisome = smelly

BENEDICK Thou hast frighted the word out of his right sense, so forcible is thy wit. But I must tell thee plainly, Claudio undergoes my challenge, and either I must shortly hear from him, or I will subscribe him a coward. And, I pray thee now, tell me for which of my bad parts didst thou first fall in love with me? 55

51-54 "Your wit is so powerful, you've frightened the word out of its true meaning. But I will tell you in plain words, that I have made my challenge to Claudio, and either he will accept it very soon, or I will declare him a coward."

BEATRICE For them all together, which maintained so politic a state of evil that they will not admit any good part to intermingle with them. But for which of my good parts did you first suffer love for me? 60

57-59 "For all your parts as a whole, which add up to such a sharp state of evil that they leave no space for any good part to be mixed in."

BENEDICK Suffer love! A good epithet! I do suffer love indeed, for I love thee against my will.

BEATRICE In spite of your heart, I think. Alas, poor heart! If you spite it for my sake, I will spite it for yours, for I will never love that which my friend hates. 65

BENEDICK Thou and I are too wise to woo peaceably.

66 "You and I are too clever to be soppy lovers."

BEATRICE It appears not in this confession. There's not one wise man among twenty that will praise himself.

67 "Your words mean we can't be wise."

BENEDICK An old, an old instance, Beatrice, that lived in the time of good neighbours. If a man do not erect in this age his own tomb ere he dies, he shall live no longer in monument than the bell rings and the widow weeps. 70

69-73 "That's an example from the old days Beatrice, when people were kinder to each other. Nowadays, if a man doesn't build his own tomb before he dies, he'll be forgotten as soon as his funeral is over."

BEATRICE And how long is that, think you?

BENEDICK Question: why, an hour in clamour and a quarter in rheum. Therefore is it most expedient for the wise, if Don Worm, his conscience, find no impediment to the contrary, to be the trumpet of his own virtues, as I am to myself. So much for praising myself, who, I myself will bear witness, is praiseworthy: and now tell me, how doth your cousin? 75 80

75-79 "You may well ask: an hour of loud weeping, and a quarter of an hour of sniffling. So it's most sensible for a wise person, if his conscience lets him, to advertise his own good points."

BEATRICE Very ill.

BENEDICK And how do you?

BEATRICE Very ill too.

BENEDICK Serve God, love me and mend. There will I leave you too, for here comes one in haste. 85

Enter URSULA

URSULA Madam, you must come to your uncle. Yonder's old coil at home. It is proved my Lady Hero hath been falsely accused, the Prince and Claudio mightily abused, and Don John is the author of all, who is fled and gone. Will you come presently? 90

87-91 "There's a right old hoo-ha going on in the house. It's been proved that it was all lies about Hero, that Don Pedro and Claudio have fallen for a dirty trick, and that Don John's to blame for it all, and he's done a runner. Will you come in now?"

BEATRICE Will you go hear this news, signior?

BENEDICK I will live in thy heart, die in thy lap, and be buried in thy eyes; and moreover I will go with thee to thy uncle's. 95

Exeunt

Act 5, Scene 2

Claudio hangs his little poem on what he thinks is Hero's tomb, then sets off to marry the girl he thinks is Hero's cousin. Sucker!

tapers = candles

the monument of Leonato = Leonato's family tomb

guerdon = repayment, compensation

slew = killed

23 "I'll repeat this ceremony every year."

25-27 "The wolves have finished hunting for the night, and you can see the dawn."

Pheobus = Apollo, the Greek sun god who drove a chariot across the sky

several = separate
weeds = clothes

32-33 "Now let Hymen, the goddess of marriage, help us reach a better result than the one we have been grieving over here."

ACT 5 SCENE 3
A church

Enter DON PEDRO, CLAUDIO and three or four with tapers

CLAUDIO Is this the monument of Leonato?

LORD It is, my lord.

CLAUDIO *(reading out of a scroll)*
    Done to death by slanderous tongues
    Was the Hero that here lies.
    Death, in guerdon of her wrongs,   5
    Gives her fame which never dies.
    So the life that died with shame
    Lives in death with glorious fame.
(hangs up the scroll)
    Hang thou there upon the tomb,
    Praising her when I am dumb.   10
    Now, music, sound, and sing your solemn hymn.

BALTHASAR *(sings)* *Pardon, goddess of the night,*
    Those that slew thy virgin knight;
    For the which, with songs of woe,
    Round about her tomb they go.   15
    Midnight, assist our moan,
    Help us to sigh and groan
    Heavily, heavily.
    Graves, yawn and yield your dead,
    Till death be uttered   20
    Heavily, heavily.

CLAUDIO Now, unto thy bones good night!
    Yearly will I do this rite.

DON PEDRO Good morrow, masters — put your torches out.
    The wolves have preyed, and look, the gentle day,   25
    Before the wheels of Phoebus, round about
    Dapples the drowsy east with spots of grey.
    Thanks to you all, and leave us. Fare you well.

CLAUDIO Good morrow, masters — each his several way.

DON PEDRO Come, let us hence, and put on other weeds,   30
    And then to Leonato's we will go.

CLAUDIO And Hymen now with luckier issue speed's
    Than this for whom we rendered up this woe!

Exeunt

ACT 5 SCENE 4

A room in Leonato's house

Enter LEONATO, ANTONIO, BENEDICK, BEATRICE,
MARGARET, URSULA, FRIAR FRANCIS *and* HERO

FRIAR FRANCIS Did I not tell you she was innocent?

LEONATO So are the Prince and Claudio, who accused her
Upon the error that you heard debated.
But Margaret was in some fault for this,
Although against her will, as it appears   5
In the true course of all the question.

ANTONIO Well, I am glad that all things sort so well.

BENEDICK And so am I, being else by faith enforced
To call young Claudio to a reckoning for it.

LEONATO Well, daughter, and you gentlewomen all,   10
Withdraw into a chamber by yourselves,
And when I send for you, come hither masked.

Exeunt ladies

The Prince and Claudio promised by this hour
To visit me. You know your office, brother:
You must be father to your brother's daughter   15
And give her to young Claudio.

ANTONIO Which I will do with confirmed countenance.

BENEDICK Friar, I must entreat your pains, I think.

FRIAR FRANCIS To do what, signior?

BENEDICK To bind me, or undo me — one of them.   20
Signior Leonato, truth it is, good signior,
Your niece regards me with an eye of favour.

LEONATO That eye my daughter lent her. 'Tis most true.

BENEDICK And I do with an eye of love requite her.

LEONATO The sight whereof I think you had from me,   25
From Claudio and the Prince: but what's your will?

BENEDICK Your answer, sir, is enigmatical,
But, for my will, my will is your good will
May stand with ours, this day to be conjoined
In the state of honourable marriage,   30
In which, good friar, I shall desire your help.

LEONATO My heart is with your liking.

FRIAR FRANCIS And my help.
Here comes the Prince and Claudio.

Enter DON PEDRO *and* CLAUDIO *and two or three others*

DON PEDRO Good morrow to this fair assembly.   35

LEONATO Good morrow, Prince; good morrow, Claudio.
We here attend you. Are you yet determined
Today to marry with my brother's daughter?

CLAUDIO I'll hold my mind, were she an Ethiope.

LEONATO Call her forth, brother — here's the friar ready. 40

Exit ANTONIO

2-6 "The Prince and Claudio, who accused her of the wrong-doing you heard us speak of, are innocent too. Margaret was a little bit to blame, although it seems that it was against her will."

sort = are turning out

8-9 "Me too, otherwise I would have been honour-bound to fight young Claudio over it."

10-12 "Right ladies, off you go into another room, and when I send for you, come back in wearing masks."

13-16 "The Prince and Claudio are supposed to be here any minute. You know what to do, brother: pretend to be father to Hero and give her away to young Claudio."

confirmed countenance = serious expression

18 "I need to ask you a favour."

20-22 "To make me, or break me — one of the two. Leonato, the truth is that your niece Beatrice rather likes the look of me."

23 "My daughter taught her to look like that. It's true."

24 "And I feel the same way about her."

25-26 "I think you got that idea from me, Claudio and Don Pedro: but what is it you want to do?"

enigmatical = mysterious

28-30 "I want to marry Beatrice and I hope you'll wish us well."

37-38 "We're waiting for you. Are you still prepared to marry my brother's daughter today?"

39 "I'll do as I've promised, even if she's Ethiopian." Ethiopia was a semi-mythical place for people alive in Shakespeare's time — it's a bit like saying 'even if she's a Martian'. Hmm. It's still a bit of a racist thing to say. Shakespeare may have been 'Man of the Millenium' but he had his faults.

64

44-48 *The 'savage bull' is Taurus, the star sign for May (following on from Don Pedro's comment about February). In Roman myth, Jove, the king of the gods, turned himself into a bull to seduce a girl called Europa. Claudio's saying Benedick doesn't have to be worried about getting married and having an unfaithful wife — he can be a successful lover like Jove. Claudio is joking with Benedick.*

49-52 *"When Jove was a bull, he had a lovely bellow, and it seems some bull mated with your father's cow, and produced a calf a lot like you, because you bellow in just the same way."*

Who's the daddy?

defiled = *disgraced*

maid = *virgin*

68 *"She was only dead, so long as the lies about her were still believed."*

69-73 *"I'll answer all your questions after the service, when I'll give you all the details of lovely Hero's death. In the meantime just take it all for granted and let's go into the chapel."*

well-nigh = *just about*

DON PEDRO   Good morrow, Benedick. Why, what's the
                                                    matter,
    That you have such a February face,
    So full of frost, of storm and cloudiness?

CLAUDIO   I think he thinks upon the savage bull.
    Tush, fear not, man, we'll tip thy horns with gold   45
    And all Europa shall rejoice at thee,
    As once Europa did at lusty Jove,
    When he would play the noble beast in love.

BENEDICK   Bull Jove, sir, had an amiable low,
    And some such strange bull leaped your father's cow,   50
    And got a calf in that same noble feat
    Much like to you, for you have just his bleat.

                Re-enter ANTONIO, *with the ladies masked*

CLAUDIO   For this I owe you. Here comes other reck'nings.
    Which is the lady I must seize upon?

ANTONIO   This same is she, and I do give you her.   55

CLAUDIO   Why, then she's mine. Sweet, let me see your
    face.

LEONATO   No, that you shall not, till you take her hand
    Before this friar and swear to marry her.

CLAUDIO   Give me your hand before this holy friar.   60
    I am your husband, if you like of me.

HERO   And when I lived, I was your other wife, *(unmasking)*
    And when you loved, you were my other husband.

CLAUDIO   Another Hero!

HERO   Nothing certainer.
    One Hero died defiled, but I do live,   65
    And surely as I live, I am a maid.

DON PEDRO   The former Hero! Hero that is dead!

LEONATO   She died, my lord, but whiles her slander lived.

FRIAR FRANCIS   All this amazement can I qualify,
    When after that the holy rites are ended,   70
    I'll tell you largely of fair Hero's death.
    Meantime let wonder seem familiar,
    And to the chapel let us presently.

BENEDICK   Soft and fair, friar. Which is Beatrice?

BEATRICE *(unmasking)*   I answer to that name. What is
                                                    your will? 75

BENEDICK   Do not you love me?

BEATRICE   Why, no, no more than reason.

BENEDICK   Why, then your uncle and the Prince and Claudio
    Have been deceived — they swore you did.

BEATRICE   Do not you love me?

BENEDICK   Troth, no, no more than reason.

BEATRICE   Why, then my cousin, Margaret, and Ursula   80
    Are much deceived, for they did swear you did.

BENEDICK   They swore that you were almost sick for me.

BEATRICE   They swore that you were well-nigh dead for me.

Act 5, Scene 4

BENEDICK   'Tis no such matter. Then you do not love me?

BEATRICE   No, truly, but in friendly recompense.   85

LEONATO   Come, cousin, I am sure you love the gentleman.

> 85 "Only as a friend."

CLAUDIO   And I'll be sworn upon't that he loves her,
For here's a paper written in his hand,
A halting sonnet of his own pure brain,
Fashioned to Beatrice.

> halting = clumsy
>
> fashioned to = created for

HERO   And here's another   90
Writ in my cousin's hand, stolen from her pocket,
Containing her affection unto Benedick.

BENEDICK   A miracle! Here's our own hands against our
hearts. Come, I will have thee, but, by this light, I take
thee for pity.   95

> 94-95 "Come on, I'll marry you, but only because I feel sorry for you."

BEATRICE   I would not deny you, but, by this good day, I
yield upon great persuasion, and partly to save your life,
for I was told you were in a consumption.

> 96-98 "I won't turn you down, but I swear I'm only giving in after some serious persuasion, and partly to save your life, because I was told you were wasting away."

BENEDICK   Peace! I will stop your mouth. *(kisses her)*

DON PEDRO   How dost thou, Benedick, the married man?   100

BENEDICK   I'll tell thee what, Prince; a college of wit-
crackers cannot flout me out of my humour. Dost thou
think I care for a satire or an epigram? No. If a man
will be beaten with brains, a' shall wear nothing
handsome about him. In brief, since I do purpose to   105
marry, I will think nothing to any purpose that the world
can say against it, and therefore never flout at me for
what I have said against it, for man is a giddy thing, and
this is my conclusion. For thy part, Claudio, I did think
to have beaten thee, but in that thou art like to be my   110
kinsman, live unbruised and love my cousin.

> 101-102 "A whole college of wise-crackers couldn't taunt me out of my good mood."
>
> satire = witty poem
>
> epigram = witty comment
>
> 105-109 "Since I plan to marry, I won't listen to criticism, so don't tease me for what I've said about marriage in the past, because men do change their minds, and that's all there is to it."
>
> kinsman = relative

CLAUDIO   I had well hoped thou wouldst have denied
Beatrice, that I might have cudgelled thee out of thy
single life, to make thee a double-dealer, which, out of
question, thou wilt be, if my cousin do not look   115
exceeding narrowly to thee.

> 112-116 "I was hoping you'd turn Beatrice down so I'd have an excuse to beat you out of your single life, to make you a married man, which you certainly will be unless Beatrice turns against you."

BENEDICK   Come, come, we are friends. Let's have a
dance ere we are married, that we may lighten our own
hearts and our wives' heels.

LEONATO   We'll have dancing afterward.   120

> 123-124 "There's no better walking stick than one with a horn handle."

BENEDICK   First, of my word! Therefore play, music.
Prince, thou art sad. Get thee a wife, get thee a wife!
There is no staff more reverend than one tipped with
horn.

Enter a Messenger

MESSENGER   My lord, your brother John is ta'en in flight,   125
And brought with armed men back to Messina.

BENEDICK   Think not on him till tomorrow.
I'll devise thee brave punishments for him.
Strike up, pipers.

Dance

Exeunt

> And they all lived happily ever after...

> Yuk. I hate happy endings.

> 125-126 "Your brother John has been captured as he tried to escape, and brought back to Messina under armed guard."

Act 5, Scene 4

Act 5 — Revision Summary

Not so fast... I saw you thinking about skipping this page. It may be the last one in the book, but that doesn't make it any less useful than all the others. If you were the youngest child in the family, how would you feel if your parents never spoke to you? If you were the last person to get into the lunch queue, how would you feel if the dinner ladies refused to feed you? Not that great, let's be honest. Think of a poor page's feelings — read it properly from top to bottom and answer all the questions. You'll sleep easier at night and you never know, it might even get you better marks.

SCENE 1

1) Why is Antonio worried about Leonato?

2) Leonato won't listen to Antonio's advice. Who does he say he would take advice from?

3) Does Leonato think philosophers are good or bad at dealing with toothache?

4) In lines 41 to 44 does Leonato think Hero is guilty or innocent?

5) What does Leonato say he wants to do with Claudio, despite the fact he's an old man?

6) Describe Claudio based on lines 76 and 77.

7) What's "foining fence" (line 85)?

8) In lines 105 to 107 does Don Pedro think Hero is guilty or innocent?

9) What does Don Pedro say Benedick was almost in time for (lines 116 to 117)?

10) Claudio says he and Don Pedro were looking for Benedick so he could cheer them both up. Why was that a mistake?

11) Benedick whispers his challenge to Claudio. Write down the exact lines where he makes his challenge.

12) Who does Benedick call "Lord Lackbeard"? What does he mean?

13) In lines 200 to 201, what makes Don Pedro realise he may have been tricked?

14) Don Pedro calls Dogberry "this learned constable". Do you think he means it?

15) Who admits to the trick?

16) Write down the words Claudio says that tell you he doesn't believe the stories about Hero any more.

17) When Borachio says everything was his fault, Leonato disagrees. Who else does he say is to blame?

18) What does Leonato ask Claudio to do to make up for his mistake?

SCENE 2

19) Who does Benedick ask to fetch Beatrice?

20) What is Benedick having trouble doing for Beatrice?

21) Why does Beatrice say she won't kiss Benedick?

22) Who brings the news that the plot's been uncovered?

SCENE 3

23) Write out Don Pedro's speech from line 24 to line 28 in your own words.

24) Where are Don Pedro and Claudio going next?

SCENE 4

25) Why does Leonato tell the women to go away and come back wearing masks?

26) What does Benedick ask Leonato for permission to do?

27) How do Claudio and Hero prove that Benedick and Beatrice really do love each other?

28) Who does Benedick advise to get married?